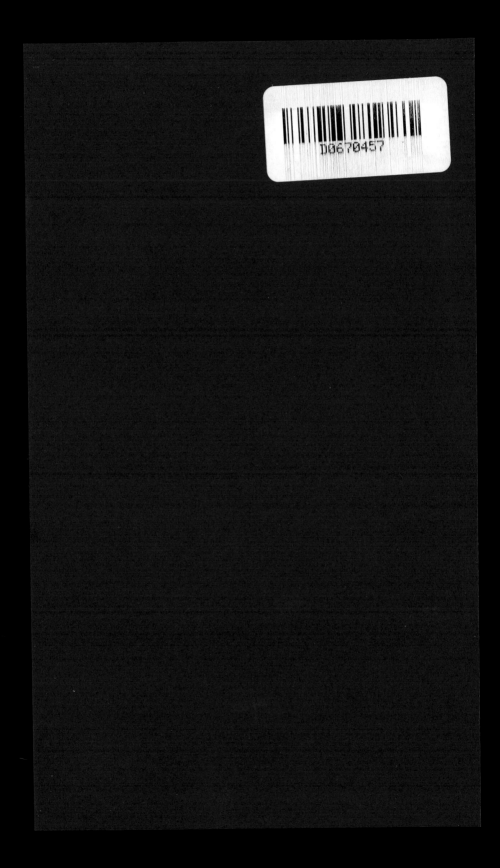

STARTING TODAY

ONE MINUTE BIBLE

STARTING TODAY

ONE MINUTE BIBLE

*Scriptures and Stories
for the Daily Grind*

RUBEL SHELLY

BROADMAN
&HOLMAN

Nashville, Tennessee

STARTING TODAY

by Rubel Shelly

Copyright © 2001

Broadman & Holman Publishers • Nashville, Tennessee

ISBN 0-8054-3780-0

Printed in Belgium

All rights reserved

1 2 3 4 04 03 02 01

To

CHARLES (DOC) AND MARGARET MERRYMAN
without whom *The FAX of Life*
might not have left the drawing board

and

BONNIE CRIBBS
who created and maintains its e-mail
presence for people around the world

INTRODUCTION

When I begin a day with God, everything else about it goes better. So I value time spent in prayer. I cherish time with the Word of God. And I insist on taking time to reflect on the spiritual implications of the things I have on my calendar.

From that sort of beginning, each day comes to a more satisfactory end. When I neglect to start with the holy things of God, things seem to be out of sync all day long.

Isn't your experience similar?

The notion of putting God-thoughts and God-plans in their priority place for a disciple is the simple notion behind Starting Today. These are short devotional pieces intended to focus your mind on key spiritual insights that have the power to make your day better. They often attempt to highlight a single verse of Scripture that you can meditate on throughout the day.

These pieces were written originally for a list of people that began with 32 names and has grown to something over 7,000. Called *The FAX of Life*, they are sent out each Monday morning by fax or e-mail to greet people who want to start their workweek with holy thoughts that can encourage their lives of Christian discipleship.

In book form, more people can have access to whatever encouragement and insight are contained here. I hope the days we start with this volume will be better for our time together.

Rubel Shelly
Nashville, Tennessee
Fall 2001

EXPAND YOUR HORIZONS

The choice is yours: Live your life in a tight circle of the usual and expected, or step outside the lines and find out how much there is you don't know.

SOMETHING TO START WITH

Do you know Carmen de Gasztold's "Prayer of the Little Ducks"?

Dear God, give us a flood of water.

Let it rain tomorrow and always.

Give us plenty of little slugs and other luscious things to eat. Protect all folk who quack and everyone who knows how to swim. Amen.

From the Bible

When he heard them debating and saw that Jesus answered them well, he asked Him, "Which commandment is the most important of all?"

"This is the most important," Jesus answered: 'Hear, O Israel! The Lord our God is one Lord. And you shall love the Lord your God with all your heart, with all your soul, with all your mind, and with all your strength.'

"The second is: 'You shall love your neighbor as yourself.' There is no other commandment greater than these."

MARK 12:28-31

Don't we all tend to live with such narrow perspectives on life? Someone growing up in a small town is likely to be intimidated when going to New York or Paris for the first time. And what is true of geography is even truer of intellectual horizons! So long as one swims only in a tiny little pond, the fresh-water delights of stream, river, and ocean remain untried, unknown, and out of reach.

Jesus came to break the shackles that come from living in too narrow a spiritual world. He taught that life's most important thing is to love God with one's whole being. To lose our lives in His is to find life itself; to stay in our own little ponds of self-interest is to miss it all.

The second most important thing is to love our neighbors as we love ourselves.

When we escape our stagnant ponds of selfishness, we can learn to see others. Having seen them, we can care about them--especially the most fragile among them. A cup of water, a warm coat, the message of God's love--sharing these things with one of them counts for doing it to Jesus Himself.

So stretch the envelope:

• Read.

• Get to know people from backgrounds different from your own.

• See some places you have only read or heard about.

• Eat sushi, skydive, or do something different and exciting this week.

• Rather than being threatened by someone with an unconventional point of view, learn from him. Try to figure out how the person came to that conclusion. If you see something you never saw before, be honest enough to admit it.

Life is meant to be a high-seas adventure. What a waste it would be if you let its thrill pass you by like water running off a you-know-what's back!

Starting Right Now:
This week, I dare you:
Make a bold decision. Try something really unlike you—like this:

_____
_____
_____
_____
_____
_____
_____
_____
_____
_____
_____
_____
_____
_____
_____
_____
_____
_____
_____
_____
_____

LOVE BEYOND LOGIC

Some people have a better understanding than others of what love means.
And sometimes those who understand best are the very "littlest" people of all.

SOMETHING TO START WITH

Cute, blond, five-year-old Lindsey was a kindergartner whose parents received a phone call from her teacher. If you have children, you know the somersaults your stomach can turn when a teacher calls!

From the Bible

Dear friends, let us love one another, because love is from God, and everyone who loves has been born of God and knows God. The one who does not love does not know God, because God is love.

God's love was revealed among us in this way: God sent His only Son into the world so that we might live through Him....Dear friends, if God loved us in this way, we also must love one another.

No one has ever seen God. If we love one another, God remains in us and His love is perfected in us.

1 JOHN 4:7-9,11-12

"We made valentines at school today," the teacher said. "Most of the children made them for Mom or Dad or someone who was obviously very special to them. When I walked by where Lindsey was working, though, she had written 'Anthony' across the top of hers."

The teacher explained that Anthony was a little boy in her class who had picked on Lindsey and made her life unpleasant. "He had been told not to do it again. He had been told that what he was doing was wrong. He had even been punished for his misbehavior, but he has persisted." So the startled teacher had asked, Lindsey, "Why are you making your valentine for Anthony?"

"Well, Anthony has been mean to me," came the sweet-voiced reply, "so I thought if I made him a special card, he'd be nice!"

That sounds so much like the gospel! God has taught us, warned us, and even disciplined us. Yet we continue going our own way. So God does the sort of thing only divine character can do. He sends more evidences of His love!

In His parable of the tenants, Jesus told of a man who planted a vineyard and rented it out to people who refused to pay him his due. He sent servants to them who were beaten, treated shamefully, and sent away empty-handed. "Then the owner of the vineyard said, 'What should I do? I will send my beloved son. Perhaps they will respect him'" (Luke 20:13). It is a parable about Jesus' mission to humankind—God's determined effort to love us in spite of our rebellion against Him.

Having a hard time with someone in your life? A client? A child? An employee? Have you already tried instruction, warning, and punishment? Perhaps it is time to do something radical by imitating Lindsey—imitating God.

Starting Right Now:
Who are they—people you find the hardest to love? Put names with faces. Put love with good intentions.

_____

_____

_____

_____

_____

_____

_____

_____

_____

_____

_____

_____

_____

_____

_____

_____

_____

_____

_____

_____

_____

_____

_____

A POWERFUL LEGACY

Your past may be littered with things you're now ashamed of, but your present is filled with opportunities to be remembered for something better.

SOMETHING TO START WITH

Each year's Nobel Prizes involve an award of $1 million. Although given in five categories (economics, chemistry, physics, medicine, and peace), most of us likely think first of the Nobel *Peace* Prize when we hear the term.

But do you know the background of the world's best-known and most prestigious prize for advancing the cause of peace?

Alfred Nobel (1833-96) was a Swedish chemist who invented dynamite. During his lifetime he made millions of dollars from the manufacture of high explosives. His inventions so magnified the killing power of weapons that some trace the history of modern warfare to him.

One morning in 1888, Nobel opened the newspaper only to find an article *about his death!* In actuality, it was Alfred's brother who had died; however, a careless editor had accidentally run the obituary for the more famous Nobel. What a great shock––and revelation––the experience proved to be! Alfred Nobel was afforded the opportunity to see himself through the eyes of his peers.

From the Bible

I hope in the Lord Jesus to send Timothy to you soon so that I also may be encouraged when I hear news about you.

For I have no one else like-minded who will genuinely care about your interests; all seek their own interests, not those of Jesus Christ.

But you know his proven character, because he has served with me in the gospel ministry like a son with a father.

Therefore, I hope to send him as soon as I see how things go with me.

PHILIPPIANS 2:19-23

Much to his chagrin, the article about Nobel portrayed him as the "Dynamite King" and let him know that he would be remembered as a merchant of death who made a fortune by making war more destructive. His legacy to the world would be his innovations in creating more efficient methods of killing people.

Dismayed over such a prospect, Nobel determined to do something about it. Under the conditions of his will, he left more than $9 million to found five prizes which would be distributed yearly in equal parts to those who had contributed the most to helping mankind. Thus did the man who invented dynamite forever link his name to the cause of peace.

How will people remember you? As someone who loved his company and did things with his family, or vice versa? As a person of integrity? As one whose genuine faith produced the good fruit of Christian behavior? As with Alfred Nobel, you can choose how you will be remembered.

A PLACE FOR EVERYTHING

Everybody seems to know they're too busy, too far out of balance. But today is your next chance to learn that it doesn't have to be that way.

SOMETHING TO START WITH

Gordon Dahl has written this insightful paragraph: "Most middle-class Americans tend to worship their work, to work at their play, and to play at their worship. As a result, their meanings and values are distorted. Their relationships disintegrate faster than they can keep them in repair, and their lifestyles resemble a cast of characters in search of a plot."

From the Bible

[Jesus] entered a village, and a woman named Martha welcomed Him into her home. She had a sister named Mary, who also sat at the Lord's feet and was listening to what He said. But Martha was distracted by her many tasks, and she came up and asked, "Lord, don't You care that my sister has left me to serve alone? So tell her to give me a hand."

The Lord answered her, "Martha, Martha, you are worried and upset about many things, but one thing is necessary. Mary has made the right choice, and it will not be taken away from her."

LUKE 10:38-42

• *Worshiping work?* Lots of us are guilty here. When we work too many hours beyond what is reasonable, we cut off the primary people in our lives, insinuating that they lack the importance of the company, the career, or the money.

• *Working at play?* Ever see somebody play golf "to relax" only to fight the course, throw a club, and otherwise create a greater need for relaxation? Ever know anyone who built her or his life around sports or hobbies? The relaxing and recreative power of play gets lost in that sort of intensity.

• *Playing at worship?* From simply being present for a worship assembly to taking time for private Bible reading and prayer, it seems all too easy to drop God in order to save time for other things. That says something about how unimportant God really was from the start.

If your life is "in search of a plot," a good strategy is to get these elements in proper balance. Yes, you need to work, but you don't have to get so consumed with it that you neglect the significant people God has put in your life. It will also help to remember that fatigue is *not* next to godliness!

So that brings us to play. It isn't necessary to be so competitive. Enjoy tennis or the lake without having to be better than someone else. Maybe you should just watch a sunset or lie flat on your back and listen to a favorite piece of music--without feeling guilty.

Then, when the time for worship comes, be thankful. Thank God for allowing you to be productive without being obsessive, to take pleasure in His creation without being so utterly consumed by it. Acknowledge Him as the giver of every good gift that has come to you.

There's a place for everything, so long as everything is kept in its place.

Starting Right Now:
Where is your life the most out of balance? What's something you could do to move it back in line?

_____
_____
_____
_____
_____
_____
_____
_____
_____
_____
_____
_____
_____
_____
_____
_____
_____
_____
_____
_____
_____

A CHANCE TO START OVER

With every crushing blow comes this counterbalance: Whatever can be destroyed can be replaced by something new, something yet unknown.

SOMETHING TO START WITH

It was a cold December night in West Orange, New Jersey. Thomas Edison's factory was humming with activity. Work was proceeding on a variety of fronts as the great inventor was trying to turn more of his dreams into practical realities.

From the Bible

Therefore we do not give up; even though our outer person is being destroyed, our inner person is being renewed day by day. For our momentary light affliction is producing for us an absolutely incomparable eternal weight of glory.

So we do not focus on what is seen, but on what is unseen; for what is seen is temporary, but what is unseen is eternal. For we know that if our earthly house, a tent, is destroyed, we have a building from God, a house not made with hands, eternal in the heavens.

2 CORINTHIANS 4:16–5:1

Edison's plant, made of concrete and steel, was deemed "fireproof." But as you may have already guessed, it wasn't! On that frigid night in 1914, the sky was lit up by a sensational blaze that had burst through the plant roof.

Edison's 24-year-old son, Charles, made a frenzied search for his famous inventor-father. When he finally found him, the elder Edison was just standing there, watching the fire––his white hair blowing in the wind, his face illuminated by the leaping flames.

"My heart ached for him," said Charles. "Here he was, 67 years old, and everything he had worked for was going up in flames.

"When he saw me, he shouted, 'Charles! Where's your mother?' When I told him that I didn't know, he said,

'Find her! Bring her here! She'll never see anything like this as long as she lives.'"

Next morning, Mr. Edison looked at the ruins of his factory and said this of his loss: "There's value in disaster. All our mistakes are burned up. Thank God, we can start anew."

What a wonderful perspective on things that seem at first to be so disastrous--a business failure, a divorce, a personal dream gone sour. Whether or not these things destroy you depends largely on the attitude you take toward them.

• Sort out why it happened.

• Learn something from the blunders.

• Think of different approaches that can be taken.

• Start over.

With moral and spiritual failures, there is forgiveness. With the slate wiped clean, you can look forward. Be wiser and humbler in view of what has happened, but don't stop living because of it.

A key truth of the Christian religion is that our hope lies in an unseen future rather than in a wretched past.

Starting Right Now:
Have you witnessed the death of a dream, the end of an expectation? Think of what it might lead to:

_____
_____
_____
_____
_____
_____
_____
_____
_____
_____
_____
_____
_____
_____
_____
_____
_____
_____
_____
_____
_____
_____
_____
_____

FOR THE CHILDREN'S SAKE

You won't do everything right as a parent; nobody ever does. But you can make sure your children know one thing: They are loved every day.

SOMETHING TO START WITH

Some discoveries are fittingly described as "startling," "unanticipated," or "astonishing." But here's the result of a 35-year Harvard study that surely surprised nobody: *Children who sense they are loved are healthier as adults.*

Eighty-seven Harvard men were followed into middle age. Those who were healthiest at age 55 had written at age 20 that their parents cared deeply about them. Their peers who were suffering from such illnesses as heart disease and hypertension at 55 had written parental assessments 35 years earlier saying that their parents were more distant, less loving, and frequently unjust.

The link between health and love on the one hand or disease and inattention on the other was independent of such key risk factors as family history or smoking.

Another report I filed away almost a year before this one tells the same story from a very different starting point. It said that almost 70% of juveniles and young adults in long-term correctional facilities did not live with both parents growing up. It also reported that growing up in a fatherless home is judged a contributing

From the Bible

Some people were bringing little children to [Jesus] so He might touch them. But His disciples rebuked them.

When Jesus saw it, He was indignant and said to them, "Let the little children come to Me; don't stop them, for the kingdom of God belongs to such as these.

"I assure you: Whoever does not welcome the kingdom of God like a little child will never enter it."

After taking them in His arms, He laid His hands on them and blessed them.

MARK 10:13-16

factor in as many as three of four teen suicides and four in five teen psychiatric admissions.

All this combines to say that the children, grandchildren, or other valued young people in your life need your time and attention. "This is not about buying them stuff," said the Harvard psychologist making the first report cited above. "It's about accepting the child's perception of their relationship with you as the truth" and behaving so "your child may experience you as just and loving."

Don't take something so important as rearing children for granted. Don't leave it to your mate to supply what only you can give. As C. Everett Koop, former United States Surgeon General, has said: "Life affords no greater responsibility, no greater privilege, than the raising of the next generation."

Starting Right Now:
Go out of your way to express to your children how much they mean to you. Make a note of it:

_____

_____

_____

_____

_____

_____

_____

_____

_____

_____

_____

_____

_____

_____

_____

_____

_____

_____

_____

_____

_____

_____

_____

_____

NOT SUCH A GOOD DEAL

"The problem with sin," the preacher said, "is that it always costs you more than you wanted to pay and keeps you longer than you wanted to stay."

SOMETHING TO START WITH

Thirty years ago, a Frenchman named Andre-Francois Raffray made what he considered a "great deal." He agreed to pay a 90-year-old woman $500 a month until she died. In return, after her death, he would own free and clear her sought-after grand apartment in the south of France.

There was nothing illegal about Raffray's contract with Jeanne Calment. Buying an apartment *en viager* (i.e., for life) is not uncommon in France. The elderly owner receives a predictable monthly income from the buyer; the buyer gets a bargain in real estate––in most cases. Even if he pays the owner for only a few months, the buyer inherits the property upon the owner's death.

But this particular deal went sour. At one point, the *Guinness Book of Records* listed Ms. Calment as the world's oldest person able to document her age. She died at the age of 122 on August 4, 1997! Mr. Raffray, however, died on Christmas Day 1995––after paying more than $184,000 for an apartment he never lived in or owned. And under French law, his wife, children, and grandchildren were forced to continue paying the elderly lady $500 per month until she died nearly two years later.

From the Bible

Godliness with contentment is a great gain....But those who want to be rich fall into temptation, a trap, and many foolish and harmful desires, which plunge people into ruin and destruction.

For the love of money is a root of all kinds of evil, and by craving it, some have wandered away from the faith and pierced themselves with many pains.

1 TIMOTHY 6:6,9-10

The apartment in question is valued at less than half the amount that was paid to Ms. Calment. What looked like a sure thing became a misfortune of major proportion for Mr. Raffray and his family.

It sounds like some of those deals Satan offers all of us. A flirtation, juggling figures, misrepresenting a product or service––the possibilities are practically endless. And who will ever know? What will it matter? Others do things so much worse! Well, you know the rationalizations that come to mind.

Then you begin to pay and *pay* and PAY! First goes your self-respect. Then your reputation. Next goes your job or family. It seems wrong that one could be asked to pay so much for what amounts to so little. But those are the breaks of this game called life.

Integrity is better kept than recovered. So watch out for those tawdry deals that offer you what you have no right to possess. They exact much too high a price in the long run.

DID I HEAR YOU RIGHT?

*Give the mind one word, and it can create paragraphs of possible meanings.
What a waste—when all that energy can be spared with one word: "Huh?"*

SOMETHING TO START WITH

A psychiatrist, an engineer, and a doctor got lost in the Canadian woods. Stumbling onto a trapper's cabin but getting no response at the door, they went inside for shelter––and to wait for the fellow to return.

In the corner, sitting on a crude platform at waist level, was a wood-burning stove. It quickly became not only the focus of interest for their half-frozen bodies but the center of their conversation as well.

From the Bible

When [Paul and Barnabas] arrived at Jerusalem, they were welcomed by the church, the apostles, and the elders, and they reported all that God had done with them. But some of the believers from the party of the Pharisees stood up and said, "It is necessary to circumcise them and to command them to keep the law of Moses!"

Then the apostles and the elders assembled to consider this matter.

ACTS 15:4-6

The psychiatrist explained the stove's unusual positioning as evidence of the trapper's psychological problems brought on by isolation. The engineer, on the other hand, saw it as an ingenious form of forced-air heating. The physician surmised the man had arthritis and found it too painful to bend over to put wood into his stove.

When the trapper finally arrived, they could not resist asking him about his stove whose warmth they had enjoyed. "Simple," said the man. "My stove pipe is too short."

I wasn't along for that hunting trip, but I've been where those guys were that day. I've tried to read someone's mind. I've seen motives that weren't there. I've walked into situations, caught a snatch of what was happening or being said, and made a fool of myself by some inappropriate reaction. Or I've used a perfectly innocent statement or slip of the tongue as my excuse for taking offense.

I can really be a jerk sometimes!

Communication is a wonderful thing—when it happens. But there are so many barriers. Each of us brings baggage to every situation. Words can be vague or carry very different nuances for people of dissimilar backgrounds. On top of that are the prejudices and blind spots all of us have.

Lots of confusion could be eliminated and far more progress made this week by following this simple rule: *When something isn't clear, ask.* Don't assume. Don't guess. Don't gamble. Swallow your pride and say, "I'm not sure I understand. Do you mind explaining?"

This simple strategy could save you embarrassment, time, and money. More important still, it might even save some of your life's most important relationships.

RELATIVELY SPEAKING

Things could be worse. The broken glass could have flattened ALL your tires. The hot water could have gone out in the WINTER. Look on the bright side.

SOMETHING TO START WITH

A female college freshman wrote the following letter to her parents:

Dear Mom and Dad,

Just thought I'd drop you a note to let you know about my plans. I've fallen in love with a guy named Jim. He quit high school after his junior year to get married. About a year ago, he got a divorce.

We've been going steady for two months and plan to get married in the fall. Until then, I've decided to move in with him. I think I might be pregnant.

At any rate, I dropped out of school last week. Of course, I'd like to finish college sometime in the future.

The letter continued on the next page:

Mom and Dad, I just want you to know that everything I've written so far in this letter is false. None of it is true.

But it is true that I got a D in Western Civ and flunked Algebra. And it is also true that I'm going to need some more money for tuition payments.

It doesn't take a genius to figure out her strategy, does it? Even bad news can sound pretty good if it is kept in perspective.

From the Bible

Let the peace of the Messiah, to which you were also called in one body, control your hearts.

Be thankful.

Let the message about the Messiah dwell richly among you, teaching and admonishing one another in all wisdom, and singing psalms, hymns, and spiritual songs, with gratitude in your hearts to God.

And whatever you do, in word or in deed, do everything in the name of the Lord Jesus, giving thanks to God the Father through Him.

COLOSSIANS 3:15-17

How we evaluate ourselves and the people around us depends on our viewpoint.

• Today you will be tempted to feel sorry for yourself. *Don't!* Lots of people would love to trade places with you. Before you get down in the dumps over whatever is bothering you, read today's obituaries to see how many people younger than you died yesterday, or visit the burn or stroke rehab center at a local hospital.

• Today you may feel the need to whine, blame, or make excuses for something that goes wrong. *Don't!* Take steps to put things right, but avoid making yourself look small by ducking responsibility.

• Today you may be inclined to take either too much blame or too much credit. *Don't!* It may not have been your best day, but it almost surely will not have been your worst either. Submit it to God in prayer, and ask Him to make the day count for His purpose in your life.

As the day unfolds for you, try to keep things in perspective.

Starting Right Now:
For every rotten break you've gotten in the last month, think of five things that are going your way.

_____
_____
_____
_____
_____
_____
_____
_____
_____
_____
_____
_____
_____
_____
_____
_____
_____
_____
_____
_____
_____
_____
_____

INCREASE IN FACE VALUE

Do you know anyone who has those little smile wrinkles at the corners of their eyes? You know how they got there? Even their enemies know.

SOMETHING TO START WITH

Chelsey Thomas was born with a rare medical condition that impaired her facial muscles, making her unable to control them.

As a result, she couldn't smile.

When she started school, children teased this otherwise happy girl about her unusual looks. Soon she became extremely self-conscious, and her unhappiness on the inside began to match the perpetually sad look on her face.

But fortunately there was hope for little Chelsey. Doctors decided to transplant muscles and nerves from her leg into her face to try to correct the problem. The plan involved an 11-hour operation to correct the left side of her face, followed by an identical 11-hour procedure on the right side five months later. If everything went well, the surgeons would have her smiling by her eighth birthday.

As I followed the plight of this little girl without a smile, I thought a lot about smiles and the non-verbal messages they send.

Think about the difference a smile makes when your physician walks into

From the Bible

Therefore, God's chosen ones, holy and loved, put on heartfelt compassion, kindness, humility, gentleness, and patience, accepting one another and forgiving one another if anyone has a complaint against another. Just as the Lord has forgiven you, so also you must forgive. Above all, put on love–the perfect bond of unity.…

Rejoice in the Lord always. I will say it again: Rejoice!

Let your graciousness be known to everyone. The Lord is near.

COLOSSIANS 3:12-14
PHILIPPIANS 4:4-5

the examination room after reading your x-rays or looking over your lab reports. Think about the reassurance you feel when a customer looks up from your proposal with a big grin on his face. Think of the contagious smiles of children that seem to work magic on all of us.

Now think of it the other way. Think of what one of your big, genuine smiles means to your employees, a clerk at the convenience store, your customers, the people you see at the end of your day. It speaks volumes of goodwill to them. It can't be faked, though, or it won't work! And if it is the preamble to some act of genuine kindness, it can work a miracle in an instant!

Chelsey's surgery was successful, and her face now glows with a big smile. The doctors have told her parents, however, that her smile will never be completely spontaneous. She will always have to think about it to smile.

For you to smile today, you may need to think about it too. But it is a conscious choice with a predictable benefit.

Starting Right Now:
Smile for the mirror. Smile for no reason. Smile when no one smiles back. There you go—that looks better.

_____
_____
_____
_____
_____
_____
_____
_____
_____
_____
_____
_____
_____
_____
_____
_____
_____
_____
_____
_____

YOUR BIGGEST FAN

Never fool yourself into believing that your life will be easy. But never forget that you have God's strong arm around you to lead you through it.

SOMETHING TO START WITH

On the road to Olympic glory, there have been many memorable moments. And some of them have given us living pictures of what courage and persistence really means.

Danish equestrian Lis Hartel had polio in 1944 and was left almost completely paralyzed. Although she had to be helped in order to mount and dismount her horse, she still won the silver medal in dressage in 1952. That's bravery.

Rafer Johnson nearly lost his toes in a conveyor-belt accident as a child, yet this American decathlete rose to Olympic glory. In 1956 he overcame an injured knee and torn abdominal muscles to win silver. In 1960, with his training cut short by injuries from an auto accident, he still won the gold medal. That's pluck.

Wilma Rudolph, the twentieth of twenty-two children, was a sickly child. She had double pneumonia, scarlet fever, and polio as a little girl. Doctors said she might never walk again. Yet she became a track superstar at Tennessee State University and was the first American woman to win three gold medals in one

From the Bible

Therefore since we also have such a large cloud of witnesses surrounding us, let us lay aside every weight and the sin that so easily ensnares us, and run with endurance the race that lies before us, keeping our eyes on Jesus, the source and perfecter of our faith, who for the joy that lay before Him endured a cross and despised the shame, and has sat down at the right hand of God's throne. For consider Him who endured such hostility from sinners against Himself, so that you won't grow weary and lose heart.

HEBREWS 12:1-3

Olympic Games in 1960. That's true accomplishment.

But my favorite story from Olympic competition involves Derek Redmond. The British record-holder in the 400 meters was running in the semi-finals at Barcelona in 1992. Heading for the tape, he heard a pop in his right hamstring, clutched his leg in pain, and slumped to the track––as if in prayer. A man rushed from the stands, pushing aside obstacles to reach the fallen athlete. Then helping the runner to his feet, Jim Redmond took the boy's arm, drew it around his own shoulder, and the two of them made their way side-by-side to the finish line. Father and son. That's love coming to the rescue.

Are you feeling discouraged today? Thinking there's no reason to stay in the race? Showing all the signs of a spiritual cripple, ready to give up? God has come out of the stands, has become one with you in your flesh-and-blood struggles, and is going with you—together—to the finish line.

Starting Right Now:

Make a list of the things that overwhelm you. Make a promise that you won't even try them by yourself.

_____
_____
_____
_____
_____
_____
_____
_____
_____
_____
_____
_____
_____
_____
_____
_____
_____
_____
_____
_____
_____

HAVE A BAD DAY

You can count on a few things going wrong today. But even a bad day spent in Christ's protection is better than a good day trying to sort it all out alone.

SOMETHING TO START WITH

Terry Huckaby was running late and got to Miami International Airport after his plane was scheduled to leave. Rushing and still hoping its departure had somehow been delayed so he could catch the flight, he made it to the gate only to discover the plane was indeed gone.

Before trying to work out an alternate schedule, the frustrated man spun a dollar into a vending machine to make up for the breakfast he had missed that morning, only to have the machine eat it. "What a day," he sighed––out loud to himself. "I missed my flight, and now I've lost a dollar." Someone behind the counter heard him and said, "No sir, you're the luckiest man alive. We just got word that your plane went down." Sure enough, the numbers on Terry's ticket matched the sobering news. ValuJet Flight 592 had crashed moments before into the Florida Everglades, killing 104 passengers and five crew members when it nose-dived into alligator-infested waters.

So…what about *your* day?

Already off to a bad start? Maybe the alarm didn't go off and you got to work late. Or maybe you stopped for coffee but spilled it in your lap when a Neanderthal in a sports car cut you off.

From the Bible

Jesus responded to them, "Do you now believe?

"Look: An hour is coming, and has come, when you will be scattered each to his own home, and you will leave Me alone. Yet I am not alone, because the Father is with Me.

"I have told you these things so that in Me you may have peace. In the world you have suffering. But take courage! I have conquered the world."

JOHN 16:31-33

Frustrated with a customer's complaint left over from last Thursday? Hey, just be thankful you have a complaint to handle. Some companies have gone bankrupt since last Thursday. And somebody who took a complaint last Thursday died since then of a heart attack.

Feeling guilty about snapping at your wife or husband this morning? Okay, so now your mate knows you're human! I'll bet it came as no surprise. The surprise might be if you were to call right now to apologize--and make a dinner date for tonight.

Like the guy who missed his plane and lost his dollar in a matter of minutes only to find out it wasn't such a "bad day" after all, maybe you need to put a few things in perspective before going further into your day.

Take a deep breath. Lighten up. The attitude you take to your next duty, challenge, or customer could improve considerably just by thinking about what could have been—but wasn't.

Starting Right Now:
Think of some people who are having a really bad day. Pray for them. Call them up. You'll feel better.

DELIBERATE KINDNESS

Some people do kind things because it makes them feel better about them-selves. Believers in Christ should be kind because that's who they really are.

"Practice Random Acts of Kindness" is the appeal these days. A quarter in an expired parking meter as you walk by, an anonymous $50 bill to a friend recently out of a job, showing up to work one Saturday at a Habitat for Humanity building site, visiting a nursing home––these are all acts of kindness, all right.

But why should kind behaviors be *random?* My dictionary defines the word to mean "having no specific pattern or objective; lacking causal relationships; haphazard." Anyone will be kind occasionally. Shouldn't people be able to *count* on your kindness rather than be *surprised* by it?

Jesus wasn't acting on a whim when he asked to eat with Lazarus. He didn't do anything out of character by healing a blind man at Jericho. To those who really knew Him, it was not bizarre that He defended the dignity (and life!) of a woman caught in adultery. In all these situations, He was doing exactly what we would expect Him to do.

This kindness is also a defining feature of someone who *follows* Jesus Christ.

From the Bible

The apostles gathered around Jesus and reported to Him all that they had done and taught. He said to them, "Come away by yourselves to a remote place and rest a little."…

But many saw them leaving and recognized them. They ran there on foot from all the towns and arrived ahead of them. So as He stepped ashore, He saw a huge crowd and had compassion on them, because they were like sheep without a shepherd. Then He began to teach them many things.

MARK 6:30-31,33-34

It is part of what Galatians 5:22-23 calls the "fruit of the Spirit." According to First Corinthians 13, it is a behavior that displays God's love.

Don't misunderstand my point. I'm not against kindness wherever it is found. But I'd sure like to think that when the person in front of me in line is treated with kindness, I can expect the same brand of courtesy when it's my turn. I'd hate to find out that the store cashier was acting randomly--and, wouldn't you know it, she had done her kind, random deed just before dealing with me!

Clients and customers want you to be kind to them this week. Friends and family need your kindness even more. So don't make them wonder, bide their time, and hope to be lucky enough to catch you in a good mood. Let them learn that you can be counted on for kindness. Make it your standard operating procedure. Let it be the pattern of your life.

Starting Right Now:
Instead of waiting on a whim of emotion, why not go ahead and plan a few kindnesses for today?

_____

_____

_____

_____

_____

_____

_____

_____

_____

_____

_____

_____

_____

_____

_____

_____

_____

_____

_____

_____

_____

_____

WHAT'S YOUR EXCUSE?

When problems arise, there's usually enough blame to go around.
Are you the first one to cover your tail, or to admit you made a mistake?

SOMETHING TO START WITH

Here are some cases of actual written excuses turned in to teachers in Albuquerque, New Mexico, by parents on behalf of their children:

- "Please excuse Sara for being absent. She was sick and I had her shot."
- "Please excuse Johnnie for being. It was his father's fault."
- "Please excuse Ray from school on Friday. He has very loose vowels."

From the Bible

"A man was giving a large banquet and invited many. At the time of the banquet, he sent his slave to tell those who were invited, 'Come, because everything is now ready.' But without exception they all began to make excuses. . . .

Then in anger, the master of the house told his slave, 'Go out quickly into the streets and alleys of the city, and bring in here the poor, maimed, blind, and lame! . . . For I tell you, not one of those men who were invited will enjoy my banquet!'"

LUKE 14:16-18,21,24

Excuse-making seems to be an art form for some people these days. It is the rare and exceptional person who steps up at a critical time to accept responsibility when things have gone poorly.

Remember the Garden of Eden? Adam blamed Eve, who promptly blamed the serpent. Pity the poor serpent, for there was nobody left for him to blame!

One of the best qualities of strong, effective leaders is that they take responsibility for what happens on their watch. Rather than pointing fingers, they are quick to respond with action plans, to see what can be learned, to make adjustments in the way things are done. Change for the better doesn't happen when someone is more worried about fixing blame than improving the situation.

The legendary Paul "Bear" Bryant coached Alabama football teams to winning season after winning season, including national championships. He once explained his theory of how to build a successful team: "I'm just a plowhand from Arkansas," Coach Bryant said, "but I have learned how to hold a team together––how to lift some men up, how to calm others down, until finally they've got one heartbeat together. There's just three things I'd ever say: 'If anything goes bad, *I* did it; if anything goes semi-good, *we* did it; and if anything goes really good, *you* did it.' That's all it takes to get people to win football games for you."

Whether it's in athletics, on the job, or at home, leaders are quick to give credit to others and to shoulder responsibility for problems. Jesus is the perfect example of that sort of leadership. He took the world's sin problem on His shoulders. It wasn't fair, but it was the only way it would work in the long run.

Anyone who is good at making excuses will seldom excel at anything else.

HOT ON THE TRAIL

Do you ever find yourself unable to keep one thought in your mind without two more crowding it out? Maybe you're too busy—or just too distracted.

SOMETHING TO START WITH

A man who had bought a new hunting dog was eager to see how the animal would perform. So he took him into the woods one day, hoping to track down and bag some really big game.

No sooner had they gotten into the woods than the dog picked up the trail of a bear. Off he went, with the excited hunter close behind. Then the animal stopped suddenly, sniffed the ground, and headed down an altogether different path. He had caught the scent of a deer that had crossed the path of the bear.

A few minutes later, the process repeated itself. The dog stopped, smelled the ground, and headed in still another direction. This time it was the scent of a rabbit that had crossed the path of the deer, and the poor pooch was sidetracked again.

On and on it went, until the breathless hunter caught up with his dog, only to find him barking triumphantly down the hole of a field mouse.

This same formula has destroyed many a business. It usually starts when a

From the Bible

As they were traveling on the road someone said to Him, "I will follow You wherever you go!"

Jesus told him, "Foxes have dens, and birds of the sky have nests, but the Son of Man has no place to lay His head."...

Another also said, "I will follow You, Lord, but first let me go and say good-bye to those at my house."

But Jesus said to him, "No one who puts his hand to the plow and looks back is fit for the kingdom of God."

LUKE 9:57-58,61-62

company loses sight of its true strengths and believes itself able to be all things to all people. A series of unwise and unrelated acquisitions later, a company like this discovers itself hopelessly diversified across too broad a range of products. It fails quickly by virtue of losing its focus, its marketing know-how, and finally its client base.

Saddest of all, the same thing has destroyed many believers who started out with high resolve to honor Christ in the marketplace, do noble things with their lives, and pursue lofty goals. Company growth, travel, money, flirtation, pride-- a series of distractions came across the trail. Each one was pursued just far enough to pull the Christian a bit farther away from what was most important.

Keep your eyes on Jesus. Set every dial to due north. And even when the directions become confusing, you'll look back and realize that you've been walking a straight line.

Stay on the upward path, and watch out for those seductive distractions.

Starting Right Now:
Invisible priorities are no priorities at all. Write your goals in black and white. Make them hard to miss.

ALL THAT GLITTERS

You're not the first one to find yourself consumed with cares for earthly things that won't matter in the end. But don't be the last one to let them go.

SOMETHING TO START WITH

Did you hear the one about the fellow who had worked so hard for so long to build a successful company and personal portfolio that he was perturbed over having to leave everything behind when he died? The wealthier he got, the more disturbed he became. So one night he prayed with unusual fervor: "God, I need to take something with me. I've worked so hard for all this stuff, so please, *please* let me take some of it to heaven."

To his surprise, he heard God's voice respond. "No," came the answer. "It is forbidden to bring things from your earthly life to heaven."

From the Bible

Instruct those who are rich in the present age not to be arrogant or to set their hope on the uncertainty of wealth, but on God, who richly provides us with all things to enjoy. Instruct them to do good, to be rich in good works, to be generous, willing to share, storing up for themselves a good foundation for the age to come, so that they may take hold of life that is real.

1 TIMOTHY 6:17-19

"But, please!" he begged. "May I bring just one suitcase with the things that matter most to me?"

"All right," God said. "But only one."

So the man set about disposing of all his holdings and converting everything into gold bricks. He packed a suitcase with millions and millions of dollars in gold and stashed it under his bed. The night came when he died, and he grabbed his piece of special luggage as he began to soar toward heaven.

An angel met him at the gate and told him baggage was not allowed. "But I have special permission from God," he said. "Just ask Him."

"What could possibly be so valuable?" the angel wondered aloud. "Would you please open the suitcase so I can see?"

With obvious pride, the man set the case down, snapped its heavy latches, and opened it. Beaming with joy, he waited for the angel's response—only to see that his heavenly greeter was perplexed.

"Pavement?" asked the angel. "You brought *pavement?!?"*

Okay, the joke is corny and the punch-line predictable. But doesn't it carry an important truth we all need to hear often? When all is said and done, things that typically get the major share of our time and attention don't amount to much.

So why do we put more effort into real estate than prayer? Why do we read more *Wall Street Journal* each day than Scripture? Why do we worry more about making money than about using what we already have to honor the Lord and help the weakest among us?

Let your family know they mean more to you than pavement. Don't get confused about what matters most in this life.

BUTTERFLY KISSES

He floated like a butterfly, stung like a bee. But there's a good lesson to learn from Muhammad Ali. And it's not what you think—just read on and see.

SOMETHING TO START WITH

Harold Conrad, a former boxing writer who came to be better known as a playwright and author, told of visiting two prisons with heavyweight fighter Muhammad Ali. "One of the prisons was for women," wrote Conrad. "All the inmates lined up, and they were ooh-ing and aah-ing as he went along. And there were some good-looking ones. But he kissed only the ugly ones."

From the Bible

"The righteous will answer Him, 'Lord, when did we see You hungry and feed You, or thirsty and give You something to drink? When did we see You a stranger and take You in, or without clothes and clothe You? When did we see You sick, or in prison, and visit You?

"And the King will answer them, 'I assure you: Whatever you did for one of the least of these brothers of Mine, you did for Me.'"

MATTHEW 25:37-40

After they left the prison, the writer asked the fighter to explain why––*if he chose to kiss any of those women*––he had picked only the ugly ones. "Because no one ever kisses 'em," responded the man who called himself The Greatest, "but now they can remember that Ali kissed 'em."

Maybe you hear in his statement just another example of Ali's pompous ego. Perhaps you're right. But in my opinion, it reflects his barely-below-the-surface memories of times and places that had been painful slights to him as a black man before he became wealthy, famous, and the object of so much attention. It is an acknowledgment by one human being of the need all of us feel for positive strokes.

Pretty girls get kissed. Straight-A students get compliments. Good athletes receive cheers. Wealthy people get perks. High achievers get citations.

But average people don't expect that kind of attention. They often don't think they're very important. Folks with average skills doing average jobs just tend to blend in with the woodwork.

Everybody needs affirmations of his or her intrinsic worth as a human being––a person created in God's image and loved by Him. Performance aside, people need to be noticed. They need pats on the back, smiles, hugs. It's how we tell one another, "Hey, you're not alone!"

When you see someone looking confused or hurt at work, make a connection. "Is everything all right? Do you need a friend? Can I help?" When you get home, remember that small children need laps, and adolescents need affirming hugs. It's a heart-warming sight to see people who've been married a long time who still hold hands when they walk along.

No person is unimportant in a world Jesus died to save.

DOING IT REGARDLESS

You don't have to say "I promise" to validate the worth of your commitments. The fact that you have spoken them at all is enough to make them stick.

SOMETHING TO START WITH

Have you noticed how people appear to be tyrannized by their feelings these days? Tell me you haven't heard someone say a line like this:

- "I'm not sure how I feel about that."
- "If he doesn't do his fair share, I don't feel I should be expected to keep my promise."
- "I know it's wrong, but I don't feel like God will fault me for what I did."

From the Bible

Dear friends, if our hearts do not condemn us we have confidence before God, and can receive whatever we ask from Him because we keep His commands and do what is pleasing in His sight.

Now this is His command: that we believe in the name of His Son Jesus Christ, and love one another as He commanded us. The one who keeps His commands remains in Him, and He in him.

1 JOHN 3:21-24

God made us in His image so we would not be ruled by our volatile feelings. He has given us the strength to do the right thing even if it means we don't exactly feel like it! And that covers everything from wedding vows to job deadlines to verbal commitments about a price. It's what makes you a person of your word.

It takes holy resolve to escape the enslavement that comes from being tossed about by whim, fancy, or feeling. So try this on for size…

- *"Today I will live in faith.* I don't know what lies ahead or what surprises may come to me today. But I know God has promised to be with me to guide, strengthen, and deliver me. By faith, I claim His promise, and I will live this day in confidence. There is nothing I will have to face that my God and I cannot handle together."

• *"Today I will live in hope.* Each day has its own supply of troublesome things, so I need not borrow from tomorrow. In fact, I rejoice at the thought of tomorrow because of the promises of God attached to my future. I will not fear failure, for God has promised to work all things for good in the lives of those who love Him. I know where my journey ends, and neither life nor death nor anything in all creation can separate me from God's love."

• *"Today I will live in love.* The bane of human life is a jealous, cynical, hateful spirit. I will not allow these negative attitudes to dominate my life. Instead, I will imitate Jesus' example of loving people-- even the ones I don't like--by turning the other cheek and returning good for evil."

Regardless of how you feel in certain situations, you have the marvelous power of choosing to live on a higher plane. So don't be ruled by your fickle feelings today. God made you for better things.

GOOD FOR WHAT AILS YOU

If you thought the only place faith had an impact was on your inner man, consider the growing proof that faith is good for you all the way around.

SOMETHING TO START WITH

Many people think there has been a bias against religion in the modern health-care establishment. Sigmund Freud called religion a "universal obsessional neurosis." A 1988 article by Albert Ellis, "Is Religion Pathological?" begins with the thesis that "devout belief, dogmatism, and religiosity distinctly contribute to, and in some ways are equivalent to, mental or emotional disturbance."

The hard evidence of science contradicts such prejudiced statements. For example, Dr. Dale A. Matthews of Georgetown University reviewed 212 studies in which faith was included as a variable. Three-fourths of those studies showed a positive effect of spiritual commitment in dealing with drug abuse, alcoholism, depression, cancer, high blood pressure, and heart disease. And the evidence only continues to grow that *religion is good medicine:*

• Dr. Nancy Andreasen, editor of the *American Journal of Psychiatry,* did work over 20 years ago that proclaimed the beneficial impact of a religious view of life for people suffering from depression.

• Religious commitment has also been found to serve as a consistent predictor of marital satisfaction, less-frequent divorce, and greater sexual fulfillment in marriage.

From the Bible

Jesus said again, "I assure you: I am the door of the sheep. All who came before Me are thieves and robbers, but the sheep didn't listen to them. I am the door. If anyone enters by Me, he will be saved, and will come in and go out and find pasture.

"A thief comes only to steal and to kill and to destroy. I have come that they may have life and have it in abundance."

JOHN 10:7-10

• A national study of adolescent drug abuse demonstrated that the single most important factor among teens who were not substance abusers was the "importance of religion" in their lives.

• Cardiologist Randolph Byrd at San Francisco General Hospital performed a double blind study of patients in that hospital's cardiac care unit. Patients were randomly assigned to one of two groups-- those receiving intercessory prayer by committed Christians unknown to them and those not receiving intercessory prayer. Neither patient, physician, nor hospital staff knew the group to which a given patient belonged. Those being prayed for had fewer cases of congestive heart failure, fewer cardiopulmonary arrests, and fewer cases of pneumonia.

Linking health and faith does not surprise people who believe Scripture, for God says, "With Me, your days will be many and you will add years to your life" (Proverbs 9:11).

So when you exercise this week, do your prayers as well as your push-ups.

Starting Right Now:
Without thinking hard, you can probably name a half dozen reasons God makes you feel better.

_____
_____
_____
_____
_____
_____
_____
_____
_____
_____
_____
_____
_____
_____
_____
_____
_____
_____
_____
_____
_____

REMEMBER TO FORGET

The next time you think forgiving someone is an optional exercise, see the Son of God hanging by His hands. And be glad He chose to forgive you.

SOMETHING TO START WITH

Clara Barton founded the American Red Cross. One day a friend reminded her of a particularly hateful thing someone had done to Clara years before. When she ignored the comment and acted as if she had never heard of it, her friend called the conversation back.

From the Bible

You were dead in your trespasses and sins in which you previously walked according to this worldly age....We too all previously lived among them in our fleshly desires, carrying out the inclinations of our flesh and thoughts, and by nature we were children under wrath, as the others were also.

But God, who is abundant in mercy, because of His great love that He had for us, made us alive with the Messiah even though we were dead in trespasses. By grace you are saved!

EPHESIANS 2:1-5

"Don't you remember that?" her friend asked.

"No," said Barton. "I distinctly remember forgetting it."

True forgiveness really does involve remembering to forget some things. Oh, it doesn't necessarily mean that you will erase the memory of what happened. That may not be possible. But to forgive someone means you will henceforth treat that person as if he had never done the wrong thing to you in the first place.

Did God forgive Saul of Tarsus for what he had done as a persecutor of His people? Absolutely. But we know for sure that God didn't lose that fact from His memory, because the Holy Spirit later moved both Paul and Luke to write about the apostle's past as a testimony of hope to others. However, we can say with the same certainty that God "forgot" what Paul had done insofar as the way He viewed him after his conversion.

When God forgave you for something you did yesterday or six weeks ago or fifty years ago, He turned loose of it. Ever since that day, He has viewed you as if it never happened. Even if you have had to live with the consequences of it, God has never once considered putting it back on your record or calling you to account for it. Even if others who say they have forgiven you have not been so gracious, God will not pull it out of a dusty file on Judgment Day. He forgave it--put it as far away as east is from west, buried it in the depths of the sea. *He distinctly remembers forgetting it.*

In the way God forgives us, we find the way to live at peace with one another. Harboring grudges, plotting revenge, and getting even are foolish wastes of time that destroy the soul.

You'll walk with a lighter step today by remembering to forget some things.

SPEAKING OF COURAGE

There is a place this side of safe where most people are content to live with their insecurities. Oh, if they only knew what it was like on the other side!

SOMETHING TO START WITH

You know the distinctive and sonorous voice of James Earl Jones. When your windows rattle at the tag-line "This is CNN," it is his unmistakable voice making it happen. Or perhaps you know his deep voice as Darth Vader in the *Star Wars* movies, Mufasa in *The Lion King,* or Othello.

What you may not know is that he suffers from a speech problem that paralyzes some people.

James Earl Jones is a stutterer.

When he was a teenager in Michigan, Jones' stutter was so bad that he hardly dared to speak. He was, as a result, incredibly shy and withdrawn. But once, in fulfilling an assignment at school, he wrote a poem that impressed his teacher. The teacher––perhaps suspecting that someone so shy and tongue-tied was not bright enough to write such a piece––decided he had probably plagiarized it. So the teacher challenged Jones to recite it from memory.

Jones was scared at the thought of speaking before the class. But he later said he thought it better to be laughed at for stuttering than to be disgraced. Amazingly, as he quoted from memory, his words were steady, smooth, and fluent.

From the Bible

Not that I have already reached the goal or am already fully mature, but I make every effort to take hold of it because I also have been taken hold of by Christ Jesus.

Brothers, I do not consider myself to have taken hold of it. But one thing I do: forgetting what is behind and reaching forward to what is ahead, I pursue as my goal the prize promised by God's heavenly call in Christ Jesus. Therefore, all who are mature should think this way.

PHILIPPIANS 3:12-15

It was then he discovered that the scripted word came easily. A career path had opened for him.

What intimidates you? What makes you freeze, become all thumbs, and stumble over yourself? Wish you could find a way to deal with it?

Well, you've driven up to automatic gates at parking lots before and seen the bar go up when your car activates a sensor near the entrance. At fifty feet, twenty feet, even ten feet away, it stays down to block your path. But as you come closer, it swings up to let you pass through. If you were to stop only a few yards from the gate, it would stay closed in front of you. Only as you move forward does it open.

If something is blocking your path to a holy commitment or worthy goal, ask God to give you the courage to keep moving ahead. The Lord has an amazing way of clearing away obstacles for those who continue to press forward.

Your responsibility is to move ahead. God's is to clear the path between you and the goal that fulfills His purpose for your life.

If we know in our heads that we often learn best by failing, then why do we live in such fear of it?

_____
_____
_____
_____
_____
_____
_____
_____
_____
_____
_____
_____
_____
_____
_____
_____
_____
_____
_____
_____
_____
_____
_____

A MORE EXCELLENT WAY

At the speed life travels these days, next month can be here before your priorities have a chance to catch up—unless your priorities are driving.

SOMETHING TO START WITH

"It's easy to make a buck but hard to make a difference."

That's what TV newsman Tom Brokaw told the 1997 graduating class at Fairfield University in Connecticut. And somebody probably told us those same words—or words to that effect—when we graduated from grade school, high school, or college. So it's time for a reality check.

How consistent have you been in living out the obvious truth that making a difference is more important than making money? Or having the phone numbers of powerful people? Or climbing the company ladder? Or getting published?

How does one "make a difference" in the world, you ask?

• *Be different.* You must be secure enough in yourself that you don't have to outperform or defeat someone else. You must understand that your own worth does not derive from what you can do, produce, or win. This sort of security comes to people who understand that their significance lies in the fact that they have been created in the image of God and are supremely loved by Him.

From the Bible

If you love those who love you, what credit is that to you? Even sinners love those who love them. If you do good to those who do good to you, what credit is that to you? Even sinners do that. And if you lend to those from whom you expect to receive, what credit is that to you? Even sinners lend to sinners to be repaid in full.

But love your enemies, do good, and lend, expecting nothing in return. Then your reward will be great, and you will be sons of the Most High.

LUKE 6:32-35

• *Think differently.* Don't see others as clients, competitors, or enemies. Don't make a big deal of gender, skin color, or national origin. Don't see black and white, rich and poor, able to pay me back and not able to return the favor. Instead, see Eleanor, Phil, Letitia, and George. See the people around you as creatures of God who deserve the same respect, fairness, and benefit of the doubt you want for yourself.

• *Act differently.* Keep your word. Pay your debts, and live within your means. Don't ask of others anything you wouldn't do yourself. Show little courtesies. Be a good citizen, friendly neighbor, and loving family member. Pay special attention to old people, small children, and the weak. Honor the Lord by putting kingdom issues first in your life and through daily obedience to His will. Serve Him by helping build up His church.

Making money is easier than making a difference, but it is the latter that defines your real stature. At the final great Graduation Day, it is the only thing that will matter.

Starting Right Now:
People who impact their world don't fit in—they stand out. What do you need to do...differently?

BOUGHT WITH A PRICE

If you have ever doubted your worth as an individual, you have never looked carefully at the cross of Christ. What more does love have to say?

SOMETHING TO START WITH

Determining the true value of an item can be tricky. In Philadelphia recently a woman spotted what she thought was an old helmet in her attic near where the Halloween costumes used to be. She cleaned it up and carried it to the Civic Center, where Chubb's Antique Roadshow was offering people free appraisals of their junk––to see if it was worth anything. An appraiser from San Francisco's Butterfield & Butterfield told her the helmet was a sixteenth century cabasset from Milan. Crafted from a single sheet of metal and covered with gold, it was valued at around $250,000.

Or try this: At the auction of Jacqueline Kennedy Onassis' personal property...

• A bundle of old magazines went for $12,650.

• A walnut humidor given to the president by Milton Berle that was estimated at $2,000-$2,500 sold for $574,500.

• Arnold Schwarzenegger paid $772,500 for a set of MacGregor Woods golf clubs and their red and black golf bag inscribed "JFK/Washington, D.C."

From the Bible

For while we were still helpless, at the appointed moment, Christ died for the ungodly. For rarely will someone die for a just person–though for a good person perhaps someone might even dare to die. But God proves His own love for us in that while we were still sinners Christ died for us!...

For if, while we were enemies, we were reconciled to God through the death of His Son, then how much more, having been reconciled, will we be saved by His life!

ROMANS 5:6-8,10

Ultimately, of course, the value of any item is market driven. No cigar holder is worth a half-million dollars, and no helmet is worth $250,000. But devotees of the Kennedy family will pay huge dollar figures to acquire ownership of their personal items. A history enthusiast will see great value in what was at one time an ordinary helmet, and be willing to pay a price far in excess of the worth of its metal content.

If you accept the thesis that an item is worth what someone is willing to pay for it, you should be flattered to learn your worth to God. For though the Scripture leads us to understand that sin has left us wrapped in the filthy rags of our own unworthiness, God in His love and mercy has chosen to bestow us with honor.

"For you know that you were redeemed from your empty way of life inherited from the fathers, not with perishable things, like silver or gold, but with the precious blood of Christ, like that of a lamb without defect or blemish" (1 Peter 1:18-19).

You're worth a fortune. Try not to sell yourself short today.

Starting Right Now:
Don't quote Christ's death from memory today. Stop and think about it, and let such love bowl you over.

SAY IT LIKE YOU MEAN IT

*Even with all the directions, instructions, and commands you have to give,
the most important words are often these: "Does everyone understand?"*

SOMETHING TO START WITH

The story sounds thoroughly made up, but it is such a good one, I like to tell it. My wife and I even use the punch line to describe a phenomenon that happens too often between us. But we'll get to that later.

Yogi Berra was burning leaves in his yard one autumn day. The wind picked up a bit, and it was getting harder to keep the fire line under control. A storage shed was beginning to be threatened, so he ran in to call the fire department.

"Hurry!" Yogi shouted into the phone. "I got a fire over here that's gettin' outta control."

"How do we get there?" the fireman asked at the other end of the line.

There was a slight pause.

Then Yogi answered, "You still got them red trucks, ain't you?"

Does that sound like some of the conversations you have with your employees? Peter Drucker claims that 60 percent of all management problems result from faulty communication.

It is always worth a little extra time to make sure the goals and methods you are trying to convey to others are clear.

From the Bible

When Cephas came to Antioch, I opposed him to his face because he stood condemned. For he used to eat with the Gentiles before certain men came from James. However, when they came, he withdrew and separated himself, because he feared those from the circumcision party. Then the rest of the Jews joined his hypocrisy.... But when I saw that they were deviating from the truth of the gospel, I told Cephas in front of everyone, "If you, who are a Jew, live like a Gentile and not like a Jew, how can you compel Gentiles to live like Jews?"

GALATIANS 2:11-14

- Talk in straight lines, not circles.
- Repeat and reinforce.
- Encourage questions.
- Go at it again from another angle.
- Ask for responses, not just nods.

Time "wasted" on the front end by talking it through carefully will be saved by not having to start over.

Maybe you've seen it happen in your church. Somebody heard something that was never said or said something that was heard wrong. Friendships were undermined. Churches have split.

Or perhaps it happened at home between you and your wife or the two of you and your child. Failure to communicate builds walls. It creates feelings of isolation and loneliness. And it can lead to relationship disasters.

When it seems to be happening between my wife and me, she will sometimes look at me, grin, and say, "Red trucks!" It's our way of calling time-out and warning us to go back to the start, to get clearer, to listen more carefully.

Keep an eye out for red trucks today. They signal mixed signals.

Starting Right Now:
What are some steps you can take in your own life to ensure your ideas get through loud and clear?

_____
_____
_____
_____
_____
_____
_____
_____
_____
_____
_____
_____
_____
_____
_____
_____
_____
_____
_____
_____
_____

TRAVELING LIGHT

Learn from those who've been slapped to the ground by the greed reflex.
Having the money to buy something doesn't mean you can afford it.

SOMETHING TO START WITH

A man hurrying through the airport was worried about missing his plane. He didn't have a wristwatch and couldn't spot a clock. So he walked up to a total stranger and said, "Excuse me, sir. Could you give me the correct time, please?"

The stranger smiled and said, "Sure thing!" He set down two large, heavy suitcases he was carrying and looked at his watch.

"It's precisely 5:09 p.m., the outside temperature is 93 degrees Fahrenheit or 33.8 Celsius, and the barometer is falling so rapidly that it is surely going to rain tonight," he said. "In London the sky is overcast and 64 degrees Fahrenheit, 17.7 Celsius. In Nairobi it is clear and 72 degrees Fahrenheit, 22.2 Celsius. By the way, the moon will be full here in Dallas tonight, and…"

The man interrupted and said, "Your watch tells you all that?"

"Oh, yes," he said, "and much more as well. I invented this watch myself, you see, and there is no other like it in all the world."

No longer worried about his plane, the man who had started the conversation said, "I'd like to buy that watch! I'll give you a thousand dollars for it."

"Oh, no," said the man with the won-

From the Bible

Then [Jesus] said to them all, "If anyone wants to come with Me, he must deny himself, take up his cross daily, and follow Me. For whoever wants to save his life will lose it, but whoever loses his life because of Me will save it.

"What is a man benefited if he gains the whole world, yet loses or forfeits himself?"

LUKE 9:23-25

derful watch, as he reached for his suit-cases to leave. "I'm afraid it's not for sale."

"Wait," said the man. "I'll give you $5,000 in cash for that watch."

"No," came the reply. "I invented this watch for my son and plan to give it to him when he graduates from college."

"I understand," said the persistent would-be buyer, "but I'll pay you $10,000! I've got the money on me, and it's all yours for that watch."

"Umm…" the stranger paused. "Did you say $10,000? All right, it's a deal!"

Delighted beyond words, the man counted out the money as a crowd gathered around. He took the watch, put it on his wrist, and shook hands with the stranger. "Thanks," he said, as he turned to leave.

"Hold on!" said the stranger, handing the man with the new watch his two heavy suitcases. "You were about to leave without the batteries."

Materialism makes some of us want everything we see. But there is an oppressive heaviness that can be avoided by traveling light.

ROOM TO GOOF UP

The best coaches know the difference between lazy, mental mistakes and misguided hustle. One shows wasted potential. The other shows possibilities.

SOMETHING TO START WITH

I listened to an executive explain to a group of about 200 interested people how he had built his dream into a successful company whose stock now trades on Wall Street. He talked about several of the things anyone would have expected––customer service, full value, meeting market demands. One item of his company policy, however, particularly riveted my attention.

As he talked about the way he treated his employees, he said, "I lavish grace on the people who work for me. I give them space for failure as we seek to improve things in the company. Experience has taught me that removing a paralyzing fear of failure from them unleashes incredible creativity and productivity."

That's the point about grace so many of us have missed. Grace is neither the abandonment of personal responsibility nor an anything-goes attitude toward faith. To the contrary, grace acknowledges that one is under God's authority and answerable to the Lord Jesus Christ. It insists on the pursuit of truth, principle, duty, and virtue. At the same time, however, it understands that no one will be saved by achieving them. Salvation is God's gift to sinners, not His reward to those who do enough.

From the Bible

"Simon, Simon, look out! Satan has asked to sift you like wheat. But I have prayed for you, that your faith may not fail. And you, when you have turned back, strengthen your brothers."

"Lord," he told Him, "I'm ready to go with You both to prison and to death!"

"I tell you, Peter," He said, "the rooster will not crow today until you deny three times that you know Me!"

LUKE 22:31-34

Part of the good news of Christianity is that God's grace gives us "space to fail" while we are seeking to bring our thoughts, words, and deeds into captivity to Christ. A performance-based religion always leaves one feeling insecure. The fear of "going to hell if I do (or don't do) this" is the primary motivation in the lives of such people. And churches filled with these people are overly cautious about everything. Paralyzed.

Properly understood, the Christian faith is based on the relationship of precious children to a loving Father by virtue of birth, not behavior. While we are trying to be sons and daughters who will make our Father happy, we live joyfully––even in our weaknesses and failures. We are secure in His love and are free to mess up without having to panic. Our churches have the freedom to explore and be creative within His pleasure.

Your Father is a better person than some people have been led to believe. What worked in one man's business has always worked in our Father's house.

Starting Right Now:
How can you creatively express to others that you accept honest errors as precursors to triumph?

FAITH IS NOT AN ACT

We can all spot the biggies who, with TV cameras shining, have been exposed as phonies. But how would our daily decisions look under that kind of light?

SOMETHING TO START WITH

Can you be bought? Would you trade your self-respect or personal integrity? What about the Faustian deal of selling your soul to the Devil?

We hear about deals of this sort all the time. A candidate is found to be lying about his war record, her marital history, or a career achievement. A student is caught falsifying transcripts and references in an effort to get into graduate school. A preacher is discovered to have a prostitute on his payroll. On and on it goes, *ad nauseam…*

Some people who make such decisions never weigh them as issues of right and wrong. They are more concerned with calculating the possibilities of *getting by* versus *getting caught.* But there is an occasional Stephanie Stephenson who reminds us that principle can still prevail.

Stephanie is 20 and dreaming of theatrical stardom. She recently auditioned for a leading role in the touring production of the hit Broadway musical *Les Miserables.* To her great delight, she landed the part. Then, only one day later, she quit and returned to Branson, Missouri, where she had a couple of bit parts in a

From the Bible

When Simon saw that the Holy Spirit was given through the laying on of the apostles' hands, he offered them money, saying, "Give me this power too, so that anyone I lay hands on may receive the Holy Spirit."

But Peter told him, "May your silver be destroyed with you, because you thought the gift of God could be obtained with money! You have no part or share in this matter, because your heart is not right before God…. For I see you are poisoned by bitterness and bound by iniquity."

ACTS 8:18-21,23

Christian musical called *The Promise* and was the understudy for the role of Mary the mother of Jesus.

In *Les Miserables* she had been cast as the modest and innocent Cosette. "Stephanie's gorgeous and talented," said the show's executive producer. "She could have played the daylights out of that role." But she gave up the part when she learned she would also have to play a prostitute in an ensemble number. In a scene called "Lovely Ladies," she would have had to wear a push-up bustier and be prodded and groped by male actors. She wasn't willing (using her words here) to "go over that line" of moral compromise.

If you find yourself in a situation of potential compromise this week, maybe it will help to remember Stephanie Stephenson's courageous example. It makes these words from Jesus leap off the page:

"What kind of deal is it to get everything you want but lose yourself? What could you ever trade your soul for?" (Matthew 16:26, *The Message*).

Starting Right Now:
Name the points in your life where, though God has your soul, ambition has your attention.

_____
_____
_____
_____
_____
_____
_____
_____
_____
_____
_____
_____
_____
_____
_____
_____
_____
_____
_____
_____
_____
_____
_____
_____

FRIDAYS WITH GOD

As a rule, we don't pray as we should. Yet as a cop-out, we often stop at praying for people without taking the bold step of serving them in person.

SOMETHING TO START WITH

Isaac Loeb Peretz (1852-1915) wrote a wonderful story of a rabbi in Russia who was greatly loved by the people and was known to have a singularly close relationship with God. Interestingly, he disappeared every Friday and could not be found for several hours. The villagers boasted that during those hours of prayer, he ascended to heaven and talked with God.

From the Bible

What good is it, my brothers, if someone says he has faith, but does not have works? Can his faith save him?

If a brother or sister is without clothes and lacks daily food, and one of you says to them, "Go in peace, keep warm, and eat well," but you don't give them what the body needs, what good is it?...

But someone will say, "You have faith, and I have works." Show me your faith without works, and I will show you faith from my works.

JAMES 2:14-16,18

A newcomer to the village was a skeptic who derided the faith of its simple people. Increasingly irritated by claims about the rabbi, he determined to find out where the old man spent Fridays. So he hid near the rabbi's house. He watched as he rose early, spent time in prayer, and left his house in the clothes of a peasant.

The young skeptic followed from a safe distance. He watched as the rabbi felled a tree and cut a great stack of firewood. He continued to watch as the rabbi made his way to a shack in the poorest part of the village and stacked the wood. It was the home of an old woman who tended her sick son. After leaving the vulnerable pair enough wood to last them a week, the rabbi quietly returned to his own home.

Peretz' story ends by telling how the man who had seen all this became a disciple of the rabbi. For the rest of his life, whenever he heard one of the villagers speak of the rabbi and tell how he ascended to heaven, he never again laughed or derided the story. He would merely listen respectfully and add softly, "If not higher."

We seem inclined to try to prove our discipleship by church membership and doctrinal correctness. That's too easy! The real proof that we know God is by loving and serving unselfishly. Food for the hungry, shelter for the cold, companionship for the lonely – this is the way of Christ. And it is also the best way to answer skepticism and unbelief.

Never do righteous acts to be seen by others, but know that your upright deeds--even the ones done in secret-- are being witnessed. If you actually know God and walk with Him, someone who is watching will discover it. That person will want to learn the secret of such a life and may come to know Christ as a result.

The best answer to skepticism is not argument but demonstration.

Starting Right Now:
Has God been bringing to your mind something you should do for someone? What is it? Go do it.

FATHER, FORGIVE THEM

Few things in American history have been as unjust as the dehumanizing of African-Americans. Yet few things are as liberating as pure forgiveness.

SOMETHING TO START WITH

When the public schools of New Orleans were integrated under court order in 1960, four six-year-old black girls were selected to break the immoral barrier that had been built over generations to keep white and black children apart. Three were assigned to one school, but Ruby Bridges was sent alone to Frantz Elementary School.

How was one little girl supposed to deal with such tension?

She was escorted to and from school each day by federal marshals for her protection. She had to run the gauntlet of taunts, curses, and threats from adults as she arrived and left each day. White parents took their children out of Frantz, and Ruby became the only child in Miss Hurley's first-grade class.

Dr. Robert Coles, a child psychiatrist, studied Ruby's experience. He visited with Ruby and her family twice every week. He interviewed Miss Hurley about her pupil. To his amazement, Ruby was sleeping soundly every night, eating well, and playing with neighborhood children as before. "She seems so happy," said her teacher. "She comes here so cheerfully."

One morning Miss Hurley was watching Ruby walk toward the school. Suddenly the little girl stopped right in the middle of the jeering crowd, and her lips started moving. Miss Hurley thought

From the Bible

They screamed at the top of their voices, stopped their ears, and rushed together against him....

They were stoning Stephen as he called out: "Lord Jesus, receive my spirit!" Then he knelt down and cried out with a loud voice, "Lord, do not charge them with this sin!" And saying this, he fell asleep.

ACTS 7:57,59-60

she was talking to them. She wondered what Ruby might be saying to people who seemed ready to kill her. The marshals tried to move her into the building, but she wouldn't budge until she had finished what she was saying.

Miss Hurley asked her about it later, and Ruby explained. "I wasn't talking to those people," she said. "I was praying for them." You see, every morning Ruby had stopped a few blocks from her school to pray for the people who hated her: "Please, God, try to forgive those people. Because even if they say those bad things, they don't know what they're doing. So You should forgive them, just like You did those folks a long time ago when they said terrible things about You." That morning, though, she had forgotten to pray until she was already on the sidewalk in the middle of the angry adults.

Think you have some tough situations to face today? Have to deal with some unpleasant superiors? Have to confront people who are unkind or unfair? I recommend you try Ruby's method.

Starting Right Now:
No need to think long about how you're being mistreated, but about how you are going to forgive.

GOD'S JUNK MAIL

If you've ever had an involuntary sigh escape your lips upon seeing the size of your in-box, think how full God's must be. And He answers every one.

SOMETHING TO START WITH

American Family Publishers must buy scores of mailing lists to pump out its sweepstakes letters. You get them. With the lure of potential millions of dollars in the game, you also get to look over their magazine bargains—— and the chance to buy a few for your office or waiting room.

From the Bible

[Jesus] then told them a parable on the need for them to pray always and not become discouraged: "There was a judge in one town who didn't fear God or respect man. And a widow in that town kept coming to him, saying, 'Give me justice against my adversary.' "...

Then the Lord said, "Listen to what the unjust judge says. Will not God grant justice to His elect who cry out to Him day and night? Will He delay to help them? I tell you that He will swiftly grant them justice."

LUKE 18:1-3,6-8

One of those lists included the Bushnell Assembly of God, and the computer apparently treated the last word of the first line as the name of the head of the household. So out went a sweepstakes notice addressed to God at the church's address about 60 miles north of Tampa, Florida.

"God, we've been searching for you," wrote American Family. The letter went on to inform Him that He was a finalist for the $11 million top prize.

One of its teaser lines spoke of the possibility that God might win the jackpot. "What an incredible fortune there would be for God! . . . Could you imagine the looks you'd get from your neighbors? But don't just sit there, God."

Now isn't that ridiculous! God having to deal with junk mail——as you and I do?

The Holy God of heaven dealing with mundane and trivial things? God having to put up with the whining, excuses, and inefficiency of people? He has no time for petty things and bumbling people.

Or does He?

Wasn't the point of the Incarnation to show that God was not distant, remote, and disinterested in our plight? Didn't Jesus have to deal with paying taxes, excuse-makers, and bickering among His disciples? And, in retrospect, don't you think a few of your prayers might have been the equivalent of "junk mail" zipped off to God?

If God knows when a sparrow falls to the ground, I think we can take heart that He is interested in everything going on in our lives. So don't hesitate to take today's stress, decision, or problem to God. And you don't have to wait for a major one. He'll be happy to hear from you about some minor annoyance as well.

It need not take long or be ceremonious. Why not do it right now? And if you've lost his address, just begin: "Our Father in heaven . . ."

ROUTINE MAINTENANCE

Many of the things that go wrong in our lives are avoidable mishaps we bring on ourselves by not being careful to keep our houses in order.

SOMETHING TO START WITH

A state-of-the-art F-117A––better known as the Stealth fighter––literally came apart in the sky on September 14, 1997. The pilot parachuted to safety, and no one in the Baltimore suburb where the plane crashed was hurt.

The specific fighter in question had been repaired and checked out thoroughly in January 1996. As part of that maintenance check, the wings were removed and reinstalled. But the inspectors apparently failed to install four of the five bolts that held part of the wing assembly in place. Two later maintenance checks missed the same problem. One of those checks was prompted when a pilot who had flown the jet reported there was too much "flex" in the wing.

Col. John Beard, head of the panel investigating the crash, said, "It is my opinion the accident was caused by unintentional maintenance oversight."

For the lack of four fastener bolts, a $42 million Air Force fighter crashed. Because of careless maintenance, the life of a pilot was nearly lost. On account of someone's "unintentional oversight," dozens more on the ground were put in jeopardy. It seems like a terribly high price for so trivial a thing as four bolts.

The same sort of thing happens all the time. A company fails because it doesn't

From the Bible

Now everyone who competes exercises self-control in everything. However, they do it to receive a perishable crown, but we an imperishable one.

Therefore I do not run like one who runs aimlessly, or box like one who beats the air. Instead, I discipline my body and bring it under strict control, so that after preaching to others, I myself will not be disqualified.

1 CORINTHIANS 9:25-27

stay abreast of market research or product development. A once-bright career goes down the tubes because an athlete didn't control his temper or because a junior executive was guilty of an ethical lapse.

Sadder still, all of us have known marriages to fail because of one or both partners' "unintentional maintenance oversight." He didn't pay attention to her. She didn't seem interested in him. Oh, there were occasional signs of trouble, but no one pursued them aggressively enough to repair the relationship properly. So one day the marriage came apart and crashed, killing both adults and kids.

And what of your personal spiritual life? A well-maintained heart is loving, joyful, and forgiving. It speaks truth and lives with honor. It longs for God as a deer pants for water in a dry place. Prayer is natural, and Scripture is precious.

It would be wise to begin today by checking the maintenance logs. Be thorough. Leave no stone unturned. And be bold in addressing the deficiencies. God wants you to fly, not crash and burn.

Starting Right Now:
There are daily, weekly, monthly disciplines you should constantly hold yourself to, like these:

_____
_____
_____
_____
_____
_____
_____
_____
_____
_____
_____
_____
_____
_____
_____
_____
_____
_____
_____
_____
_____
_____

FLYING INTO HEADWINDS

Rarely will we make significant progress in life without walking uphill and battling for a foothold. But keep trudging. The struggle builds muscle.

It was just my luck to be flying into L.A. a couple of weeks before Christmas when the fierce Santa Ana winds were blowing. On the day I arrived, a blast swept through Freemont Canyon at hurricane strength of 80 m.p.h. Trees were uprooted. Tractor-trailer rigs were blown on their sides. Roofs came off houses and landed on top of cars. I saw TV shots that night of snapped utility poles, and tens of thousands of people had their electrical service interrupted.

As we were departing Nashville for Los Angeles, though, I knew something was up. The pilot warned us that we'd probably not arrive on time. He explained that we would be flying into headwinds in excess of 140 m.p.h.!

From the Bible

Who can separate us from the love of Christ? Can affliction or anguish or persecution or famine or nakedness or danger or sword? As it is written: "Because of you we are being put to death all day long; we are counted like sheep to be slaughtered." No, in all these things we are more than victorious through Him who loved us.

ROMANS 8:35-37

Life sometimes seems that way too, doesn't it? Strong headwinds slow your progress and timing. It can be terribly frustrating. Bull markets can become bears quickly. A pleasant drive can end as a bone-crunching crash. The excitement of a child's birth can become the ordeal of her fight for life. The customary good report from your annual physical can be a physician's concern about your lab work that winds up with a diagnosis of cancer. The energy of youth eventually gives way to the limitations of age--precursors to the fact that we are dying.

Morbid thoughts these? Not necessarily. It's simply the way life works––the way it worked for our ancestors and the way it will work for our great-great-great grandchildren. Did you really expect to stay young forever? Never to get sick or have a problem? To be exempt from life's normal flow?

The next day's *Los Angeles Times* said this in a story about the winds and their havoc: "For all their destructive force, the Santa Anas did bring one holiday gift: stunning, smog-free views." There usually is a bright side to life's hurts and disappointments.

As we got airborne that afternoon, I was shocked to think about headwinds of 140 m.p.h. It made me grateful to be traveling in coach instead of up front in the pilot's seat. It would be his task to get us to our destination and land the plane safely. He did––like God always does.

If you're feeling strong head-winds today, breathe a prayer of thanks to the Lord for being in charge. Be grateful that He's God, and remember that you're not.

Starting Right Now:
The Bible teaches us to be thankful for life's rough spots. So remind yourself to be thankful for...what?

_____
_____
_____
_____
_____
_____
_____
_____
_____
_____
_____
_____
_____
_____
_____
_____
_____
_____
_____
_____
_____
_____
_____
_____

LIGHT YOUR WORLD

By now, we've seen enough school shootings and Dateline stories to make us double bolt the locks of our Christianity—just when the world needs us most.

Everybody seems to be aware that something terribly wrong and very disheartening has happened to Western culture. Statistics about crime, family disintegration, and drug abuse scare us all. Everyone either knows people who are or have been the victims of these terrible things.

From the Bible

"You are the salt of the earth. But if the salt should lose its taste, how can it be made salty? It's no longer good for anything but to be thrown out and trampled on by men.

"You are the light of the world. A city situated on a hill cannot be hidden. No one lights a lamp and puts it under a basket, but rather on a lampstand, and it gives light for all who are in the house. In the same way, let your light shine before men, so that they may see your good works and give glory to your Father in heaven."

MATTHEW 5:13-16

As to why this cultural breakdown has taken place, a statement first published in 1836 in the old *McGuffey's Eclectic Reader* seems prophetic: "If you can induce a community to doubt the genuineness and authenticity of the Scriptures; to question the reality and obligations of religion; to hesitate, undeciding, whether there be any such thing as virtue or vice; whether there be an eternal state of retribution beyond the grave; or whether there exists any such being as God, you have broken down the barriers of moral virtue and hoisted the flood gates of immorality and crime. . . . Every bond that holds society together would be ruptured."

It's obsolete to warn about "barbarians at the gates." The barbarians are on the inside, in charge, and at the gate controls.

The response to all this by too many Christians has been cringing, passive silence. We have acted as if we are helpless against the onslaught. We have given the playing field over to the enemy, surrendered our public institutions to him, and appeared to be resigned to letting him take charge. Nonsense!

Has God abdicated His throne? Has He taken back His promise of power to His people? Are lies and hatred more powerful than truth and love? *No!*

You are still called to be salt and light in this world. In this world's deep darkness, the light from even a dim lamp gives off an incredible brilliance. Others can find their way by its glow. Be aware that in your workplace, you serve Jesus first. Factory worker, professional, foreman, athlete, entertainer, president, short-order cook--you are called to model faith, hope, and love in a world that has fallen and cannot get up. Your message is that Christ lifts the fallen. He gives hope to the hopeless.

So don't give way to despair. Don't simply curse the darkness. The time has come for you to shine.

YOU CAN BE SURE OF THIS

It takes a lot of smarts and usually a lot of wrong turns to guess what the future will be like. But it takes only a little faith to know God is in control.

SOMETHING TO START WITH

Futurology is a science with very little to show for itself. Littered along the highway of human history are countless bad guesses and failed insights:

• "Everything that can be invented has been invented," declared Charles H. Duell, the U.S. Commissioner of Patents in 1899.

• Horace Rackham was advised by a president of the Michigan Savings Bank not to invest in the Ford Motor Company in 1903. "The horse is here to stay," he predicted, "but the automobile is only a novelty––a fad." Fortunately for Rackham, Henry Ford's attorney, he ignored the banker's short-sightedness and bought $5,000 worth of stock. He sold it several years later for $12.5 million.

From the Bible

We did not follow cleverly contrived myths when we made known to you the power and coming of our Lord Jesus Christ; instead, we were eyewitnesses of His majesty....

So we have the prophetic word strongly confirmed. You will do well to pay attention to it, as to a lamp shining in a dismal place.

2 PETER 1:16,19

• In rejecting a group of musicians in 1962, Decca Records made this fearless prophecy about their future in music. "We don't like their sound. Groups of guitars are on the way out." Thus the company passed on signing the Beatles.

• "There is no reason for any individual to have a computer in their home," said the president and founder of Digital Equipment Corporation in 1977.

• Clifford Roberts, founder of golf's prestigious Masters Tournament, once said, "As long as I'm alive, golfers will be white, and caddies will be black." He clearly didn't have the prescience to fore-see a 21-year-old Tiger Woods set a tournament record with a twelve-shot victory.

Humility will always be in order for us as we try to anticipate what lies ahead. But are there no certainties about tomorrow? Is there nothing on which to anchor our hope? Here are a few worth keeping in mind:

On the authority of Scripture, we can know that nothing "will have the power to separate us from the love of God that is in Christ Jesus our Lord" (Romans 8:39), that our redemption was purchased not with perishable gold "but with the precious blood of Christ" (1 Peter 1:19), and that when a Christian's earthly "tent" is destroyed, he has "a building from God, a house not made with hands, eternal in the heavens" (2 Corinthians 5:1).

Markets, trends in music, and tomorrow's scientific breakthroughs are beyond our ability to deduce. But spiritual certainties based on God's sure promises take the indecision out of today and keep us moving confidently forward.

For a secure future, put your confidence in the things of God alone.

Starting Right Now:
Make a point of believing in God's promises. Can you think of a few you need right about now?

WORTHY OPPONENTS

Your best efforts are not diminished when a competitor outperforms you.
The goal of toughness is to make you better, not to begrudge those who are.

SOMETHING TO START WITH

Mark McGwire and Sammy Sosa were not only chasing the most fabled record in American sports during the 1998 baseball season. They were also competing against each other as they closed in on Babe Ruth and Roger Maris––the only two players to have hit at least 60 home runs in a season. And no scriptwriter could have devised a movie plot better than the one that actually played itself out on September 8, 1998.

Both men were in uniform on the same field. The St. Louis Cardinals and Chicago Cubs were playing before a full house in Busch Stadium. Sosa was sitting on 58 home runs. McGwire had stroked his 61st the day before. The stadium was filled with electricity. Millions more were watching the television broadcast of the game.

From the Bible

Rejoice with those who rejoice; weep with those who weep.

Be in agreement with one another. Do not be proud; instead, associate with the humble. Do not be wise in your own estimation.

Do not repay anyone evil for evil. Try to do what is honorable in everyone's eyes.

ROMANS 12:15-17

At 8:18 p.m., in his second at-bat in the game, McGwire stroked Steve Trachsel's first pitch over the left-field fence. It was a line drive that traveled 341 feet and put the man who hit it into sports history books. And what of the man who was his closest competitor?

Sammy Sosa stood in the outfield and applauded––with a huge smile on his face––as McGwire made his way around the bases. During the ten-minute ovation that followed, he made his way in and hugged McGwire. Two athletes who respected each other for their competition shared the triumphal moment together.

Who put the adjective "cutthroat" before the word "competition" anyway? People who were stabbing their business competitors in the back. Politicians who majored in slinging mud at their opponents. Citizens whose every little squabble was judged worthy of litigation by ambulance-chasing lawyers. Angry parents who fought over the affection of their children after a bitter divorce. That's why business, government, and personal life have pages and pages of complicated regulatory legislation. And inefficiency and fear fill the lives of more and more people.

"Where do you think all these appalling wars and quarrels come from? Do you think they just happen?...You're spoiled children, each wanting your own way" (James 4:1-3, *The Message*).

Don't allow competition to make you jealous or cause you to cheat. Keep it healthy and productive by letting it inspire you to your personal best without begrudging anyone else his or her achievements.

THE DEATH OF HONOR?

Cynicism says our best days are behind us, our heroes already long dead.
But here's to heroes like you who continue to hold high the standard.

Albert Wolff died March 21, 1998, in a nursing home in Ohio at age 95. He was the last surviving member of a special group of federal agents under Eliot Ness who waged war against Al Capone.

In 1929, Eliot Ness was a 26-year-old government law-enforcement agent who set himself to smash the Prohibition-era Capone gang. He sought and received permission to form an elite unit––10 to 15 honest men––that would be above corruption in gangster-dominated Chicago. Albert Wolff served in that group, which came to be known as The Untouchables. What its men did has become the stuff of legend––in books, television, and film.

From the Bible

So they called for them and ordered them not to preach or teach at all in the name of Jesus. But Peter and John answered them, "Whether it's right in the sight of God for us to listen to you rather than to God, you decide; for we are unable to stop speaking about what we have seen and heard."…They found no way to punish them.

ACTS 4:18-21

"I always tell the truth," Wolff said in an interview after the release of *The Untouchables* movie starring Kevin Costner in 1987––one in which Wolff disputed a particular scene. "I don't just go along with things. I'm an honest man." Was he the last of his kind?

There are still hosts of women and men who "don't just go along with things." They tell the truth, keep their promises, and guard their reputations. They neither accept nor inflict sexual harassment in the workplace. They represent their products honestly and make good on their deals. They are known for their honesty.

These people go to work every day, give their best at their jobs, and sleep with clear consciences. From the money they make, they not only pay their debts but support their churches, give to the American Cancer Society, and make soccer and pee-wee baseball possible for the kids in their city.

These men and women honor their marriage vows. They take responsibility for the children they bring into the world. She feeds the baby in the middle of the night. They change diapers and wash dishes. He helps with homework. They work together to create an oasis of stability in a world of danger and distance. Most of them will never get their names in the papers, much less have obituaries in *The New York Times* like Albert Wolff. But they are the decent people who make life in this uncertain world possible.

Resist the temptation to let the daily diet of bad news make you cynical. Be grateful for good folk wherever you find them. Thank God for them. Encourage them when you can. And be one of them.

Starting Right Now:
Where has your integrity been tested the most lately? And what are you going to do to keep it intact?

MONOPOLY MONEY

To hear too many Christians talk, walking with Christ isn't half as fulfilling as big backyards, beach vacations, and basketball tickets. If they only knew.

SOMETHING TO START WITH

Children and adults like to play Monopoly. Players accumulate property, build houses and hotels, and wait for others to have to pay them for landing there. When the game is finished, the board is folded up, all the game pieces are put away, and the lid goes back on top. It has only been a game. The money won't spend.

A Rolls Royce, an extravagant house, and a more-is-better approach to life will yield no more joy for eternity than winning at Monopoly. When your life is over, when the game pieces are put away, when the lid closes on your coffin, it won't really matter who owned the railroads or Boardwalk. Earthly wealth doesn't guarantee heavenly treasure. Dollars won't spend in heaven.

From the Bible

"What do I still lack?"

"If you want to be perfect," Jesus said to him, "go, sell your belongings and give to the poor, and you will have treasure in heaven. Then come, follow Me."

When the young man heard that command, he went away grieving, because he had many possessions.

MATTHEW 19:20-22

Peter Marshall wrote a prayer that all of us should pray:

"Forbid it, Lord, that our roots become too firmly attached to this earth, that we should fall in love with things.

"Help us to understand that the pilgrimage of this life is but an introduction, a preface, a training school for what is to come.

"Then shall we see all of life in its true perspective. Then shall we not fall in love with the things of time, but come to love the things that endure. Then shall we be saved from the tyranny of possessions which we have no leisure to enjoy, of property whose care becomes a burden. Give us, we pray, the courage to simplify our lives. Amen."

The main character in Leo Tolstoy's "How Much Land Does a Man Need?" was told he could have all the land he could encircle on foot in one day. The man started off to claim only what he could care for and use productively. As time passed, however, he began to want more. With the day about to end, it became apparent that it would be almost impossible to get back to his starting point. Struggling to do so, he fell dead from a heart attack. Thus the only land he received was the tiny plot in which he was buried.

"A devout life does bring wealth, but it's the rich simplicity of being yourself before God. Since we entered the world penniless and will leave it penniless, if we have bread on the table and shoes on our feet, that's enough" (1 Timothy 6:6-8, The Message).

SUPPORTING ROLES

If you can shake loose from the need to be noticed, you will free yourself from one of life's heaviest burdens and become known for bigger things.

Never heard of Joe Miller? The Joe Miller who had a four-column obituary in *The New York Times*, September 27, 1998? Mr. Miller was 95 at his death and had a brilliant business career. After earning a master's degree in chemical engineering from Yale and working for du Pont, he started his own industrial paint company. The Pyrolac Corporation made him a wealthy man.

According to his obituary, Miller "made a fortune" with a protective coating for bathroom fixtures. Then he "made an even larger fortune" by developing a metallic paint that allowed the American automobile industry to make cars available to consumers in a rainbow of colors other than black. He also created a heat-resistant coating that protected the Apollo spacecraft on trips to the moon.

From the Bible

Fulfill my joy by thinking the same way, having the same love, sharing the same feelings, focusing on one goal. Do nothing out of rivalry or conceit, but in humility consider others as more important than yourselves.

Everyone should look out not only for his own interests, but also for the interests of others.

PHILIPPIANS 2:2-4

Quite an impressive career, right? But none of these things from his resumé was responsible for the obituary—complete with a 4" x 6" photo—in the *Times*. Here was the headline: "Joe Miller, Who Did His Part for Baseball, Is Dead at 95."

Baseball?

In high school, the sport Joe Miller loved above all others was baseball. And he had a big, strong friend at school who was skilled at soccer and football. The friend didn't want to play baseball. He resisted Miller's pressure to take it up.

When he finally did, however, he learned quickly and soon outstripped his friend. He went on to have one of the most fabled careers in baseball history, playing in 2,130 consecutive games—a record that stood until Cal Ripken Jr. broke it in 1995.

That's right. Joe Miller introduced Lou Gehrig to baseball! But chances are that you had never heard of Joe Miller until now. So what's the point?

How do you intend to "make your mark in the world"? Must you always be out front and get credit? Are you threatened by people with more skill, personality, or promise than yourself? Your greatest contribution to the company, your church, or your world may come in your unselfish development of another person. When Andrew brought his more outgoing brother, Peter, to Jesus, he was destined to be overshadowed by him. But maybe that was Andrew's greatest contribution to the Kingdom of God.

Are you in position to be a mentor to someone? Or to introduce someone to Jesus? There would be no better way to be remembered.

Starting Right Now:
Go out of your way to tell someone that you see a lot of promise in them. Anyone come to mind?

PICTURE PERFECT

Where do you look to see greatness in this world? Same place as everyone else? Or in scenes less noticeable to the crowd, but very much known to God?

I was in New York City one weekend when two amazing things happened on the same day. David Wells pitched the fifteenth perfect game in the history of major league baseball, and Iris Perez went to church and passed out worship programs.

Yankee Stadium had 49,820 roaring fans in the stands when Wells made his final pitch to Minnesota's Pat Meares and got him to loft a routine fly ball into right field. The only other perfect game at Yankee Stadium was pitched October 6, 1956, when Don Larsen beat the Brooklyn Dodgers in Game 5 of the World Series. I watched it on a black-and-white TV at my Dad's hardware store. And I could have been in the stands for Wells' game but passed on tickets in order to catch an earlier flight home.

From the Bible

Sitting down, He called the Twelve and said to them, "If anyone wants to be first, he must be last of all and servant of all.…

"Whoever welcomes one little child such as this in My name welcomes Me. And whoever welcomes Me does not welcome Me, but Him who sent Me."

MARK 9:35,37

A church in Manhattan began assembling for Bible School and worship around 9 a.m. that same Sunday morning. My hosts and I were greeted at the door by a pleasant looking lady. She spoke, welcomed us, and handed us a program. But as she moved back to the door of the foyer, the expression on her face changed. She looked distracted, even sad, I thought.

Between Sunday School and worship, one of the church's leaders said, "You need to know the story of one of the ladies of this church. Iris Perez' father died two weeks ago today. He preached for a Spanish-language church and fell dead in the middle of his Sunday-morning sermon. She is taking care of her mother, who is dying of lung cancer. Her daughter has chronic asthma and had to be hospitalized several days recently for treatment following a severe attack. Yet there she stands at the front door because today was her day to welcome people. I think that speaks volumes about her love for Jesus."

What is greatness in the kingdom of God? It seldom has to do with things we do in the spotlight. A clerk is patient with an unhappy customer. A customer returns change to which she wasn't entitled. A young couple honors its commitment to each other through a difficult time of stress or temptation. A lady with a perfectly good excuse for being elsewhere teaches children in Bible class or greets and hands out programs.

I'd have relished getting to see a perfect game pitched in the House Ruth Built. But I wouldn't exchange anything for meeting Iris in the House of the Lord.

MULTI-TASKING

If you're a believer, there's more to your day than your job description. Today is another chance to remember who really signs your checks.

A sign in an Atlanta business window said: "HELP WANTED. Must be proficient with Microsoft Word and must know Lotus 1-2-3. Must also be bilingual. We are an equal opportunity employer."

Shortly after the sign went up, a dog trotted inside, stood before the company receptionist, and wagged his tail. When the person behind the desk looked up, the dog walked over to the sign, looked at it, and whined. Not sure of what to do, the receptionist went to get the office manager.

The manager looked at the dog and looked at the sign. She was surprised, to say the least. The dog looked so determined, however, that she led the pooch into her office. The dog jumped on a chair and stared at the manager.

"I can't hire you," the manager said. "The sign says you must be good with Microsoft Word." The dog jumped down, went to the computer, and proceeded to type and print out an error-free letter. He picked up the page, delivered it to the manager, and jumped back on the chair. The manager was impressed.

"But the sign says you must know Lotus 1-2-3." At that, the dog returned to the computer. He entered data, printed a copy, and gave a flawless piece of work to the stunned woman at the desk.

From the Bible

Even if you should suffer for righteousness, you are blessed. "Do not fear what they fear or be disturbed," but set apart the Messiah as Lord in your hearts, and always be ready to give a defense to anyone who asks you for a reason for the hope that is in you. However, do this with gentleness and respect, keeping your conscience clear.

1 PETER 3:14-16

The dumbfounded manager looked at the dog and said, "It is obvious that you are brilliant and have some most unusual skills. Yet I still can't give you the job." The dog jumped down and put his paw on the sentence that claimed the company was an equal opportunity employer.

"Yes," the manager replied, "but that sign also says you must be bilingual."

The dog looked her directly in the eye and said, "Meow!"

No matter what skills you bring to the marketplace, you too must be bilingual in order to represent Jesus there. You must not only be a good administrator, sales person, or bookkeeper. You must also speak heaven's language on Earth. A Christian speaks the divine language of integrity, sincerity, and compassion. She is a person of principle without being self-righteous. He is a genuine human being who treats people with respect.

One who follows Jesus cares about others and treats them as she wants to be treated. These things aren't just "good company policy." They are basic Christian character.

Starting Right Now:
What keeps you from making Christ the Lord of your day? And what will you do to correct it?

_____
_____
_____
_____
_____
_____
_____
_____
_____
_____
_____
_____
_____
_____
_____
_____
_____
_____
_____
_____
_____
_____
_____

RIGHTLY RELATED

The church across the street is more than a building and a doctrinal stance.
It is comprised of people who share a common Lord and lineage with you.

SOMETHING TO START WITH

Joie Giese and Merrilee Woeber had worked together for three years at MCI Telecommunications. One day, in one of those unusual yet ordinary office conversations, several of their co-workers were comparing complexions. Someone guessed that Giese was Italian because of her olive skin.

From the Bible

I, therefore, the prisoner in the Lord, urge you to walk worthy of the calling you have received, with all humility and gentleness, with patience, accepting one another in love, diligently keeping the unity of the Spirit with the peace that binds us.

There is one body and one Spirit, just as you were called to one hope at your calling; one Lord, one faith, one baptism, one God and Father of all, who is above all and through all and in all.

EPHESIANS 4:1-6

"Not me. I was a Dunn. I must be Irish," Giese said. Woeber said she too was a Dunn and joked, "Maybe we're cousins."

The two women and a dozen of their peers had a good laugh––until Giese set about to clear up the matter by telling Woeber that her birth mother's name was *Lenore* Dunn. That was the name of Woeber's mother too! "There were about twelve people sitting around with their mouths dropped down to their knees," recalled Giese. Coincidence or a discovery?

Joie Giese and Merrilee Woeber soon found out they *were* sisters––separated by adoption fifty years earlier.

"We're still shocked," Giese said. "We're totally numb from it. I think Someone said it's time that you find each other. That can be the only way that something like this could possibly happen."

Some of us have more siblings than we were raised to know. We were reared Catholic or Protestant, Presbyterian or Church of Christ, Pre-Tribulationist or Post-Tribulationist. What a shame that more of us weren't raised simply to be *Christians* and to affirm the larger Body of Christ rather than just our own inherited or chosen franchises within it.

For the sake of civility and mutual respect in a fragmented world, all of us would do well to see ourselves––Jews, Buddhists, Muslims, Christians, atheists, whatever––as members of the one human family. We who wear the name of Jesus Christ should remember His prayer for those who believe in Him to be one for the sake of witnessing to the world (see John 17:20-23).

"The last thing I thought is that my sister would be sitting just outside my door," said Joie Giese. Perhaps you should look around your workplace, your neighborhood, and your world. You may be missing the joy of knowing the rest of the Family of God.

God would be delighted for you to find a few long-lost siblings.

Starting Right Now:
Get to know someone who believes differently than you—not to argue, but to understand, to unite.

ASLEEP AT THE WHEEL

Strange how many people embark on something as serious as life, thinking it will just work itself out somehow without any thought or effort. Strange...

SOMETHING TO START WITH

A 77-year-old retiree in Palm Harbor, Florida, has a habit of sleepwalking. He recently woke up to find his legs stuck in mud and his eyes staring into the faces of several alligators. A police officer who helped extricate him from his peril said he saw eight to ten of the dangerous reptiles only a few feet from James Currens––who fended off the alligators by poking at them with his cane.

How did he get in such a predicament? He sleepwalked out his door, stumbled down an embankment, and didn't wake up until he was dangerously stuck in an alligator-infested pond. A neighbor heard him hollering for help and called police around 5 a.m.

From the Bible

What makes everything clear is light. Therefore it is said: "Get up, sleeper, and rise up from the dead, and the Messiah will shine on you."

Pay careful attention, then, to how you walk–not as unwise people but as wise–making the most of the time, because the days are evil.

EPHESIANS 5:14-16

I've known a few people who were sleepwalkers. At camp and in the dorm, they would prowl around at night. They meant no harm. They were, after all, asleep. But they sometimes did do harm to themselves or others––especially in unfamiliar settings.

On the other hand, I've known quite a few people whose entire lives appeared to be exercises in sleepwalking. They simply weren't alert to their surroundings and opportunities. They were out of touch with their colleagues, their family, and their God.

How many companies have fallen by the wayside because markets changed and they were oblivious? Market research and sensitivity to trends among consumers are necessary for survival in today's highly competitive marketplace. One successful product can make people overconfident about the future and generate a sleepwalker's mind set.

It happens other places, too. Wives and husbands begin to neglect one another, and their sleepwalking ends in a tragic divorce! Friends assume too much and communicate too little. A precious relationship is neglected and dies! A redeemed soul whose spiritual life consists of nothing more than church attendance falls into moral disgrace. Sleepwalking again!

But we close our eyes to the obvious. We ignore warning signs. We become preoccupied with trivial things. By the time we wake up and cry out for help, it's sometimes too late. The alligators have us in their jaws and on their dinner menu!

Instead of sleepwalking through life, heed the Bible's counsel: "Get up, sleeper, and rise from the dead."

HONESTY: GOT THE URGE?

If you've ever gone easily to bed after surviving an ethical dilemma during the day with your conscience intact, you'll understand this fast-food fiasco.

SOMETHING TO START WITH

Henry Snowden pulled in to the drive-up window at a Burger King in Deltona, Florida. He ordered, paid for his meal, and eased away from the window. When he finally pulled over to eat, he got the shock of his life.

There was nothing wrong with his burger or fries. His drink was cold and good. But the clerk working at the window had shoved two bags out the window at the 31-year-old man. The second bag contained $4,170 in cash. And you thought it was *another* fast-food franchise that dispensed "happy meals," didn't you! What happened was a mistake by a store employee and a challenge to Henry Snowden's character.

From the Bible

You should no longer walk as the Gentiles walk, in the futility of their thoughts. . . .

You took off your former way of life, the old man that is corrupted by deceitful desires; you are being renewed in the spirit of your minds; you put on the new man, the one created according to God's likeness in righteousness and purity of the truth.

EPHESIANS 4:17,22-24

This particular Burger King puts its day's receipts in one of the same bags it uses for food orders. The idea is to have an inconspicuous burger bag rather than an inviting bank deposit bag sitting there in case of a robbery attempt. But the clerk working the window that fateful day mistakenly reached over and picked up both Snowden's bag and the deposit bag a store manager had just plopped down.

What was Snowden's response when he opened the second sack and found all the money? He knew that taking it back to the restaurant would be the right thing to do. "But I've got to admit, I was definitely tempted!" he said. Yet he returned the money the next morning. "I'm glad I was able to do the right thing. I feel better than I've ever felt." A good conscience will do that for a person!

How can you best foster self-esteem? One popular approach has been to lower grading standards so everyone gets A's and B's, to affirm all lifestyles as equally acceptable, and to reward incompetence as well as skill. Authentic self-esteem comes from being true to your convictions. You are made in the image of God. You feel good when you bear the divine image with dignity, but you feel terrible when you sully it with dishonor.

You'll have your own version of Henry Snowden's challenge one of these days. You'll have the chance to cover yourself by telling a lie. A customer will need a different product than the one you sell. You'll want to avoid an unpleasant topic of conversation with a family member.

Is $4,170 too high a price for a clear conscience? Ask anyone who doesn't have one, and he'll tell you Henry Snowden got a bargain.

Starting Right Now:
Most compromises start small. Is there a little one in your life you can stop before it gets any worse?

IN BURDENS, A BLESSING

Perhaps what you need in order to get your stress down is not a day off or a night away from responsibility, but a new approach to your problems.

SOMETHING TO START WITH

A grandfather clock stood for three generations in the same corner of the house. It ticked off the minutes, hours, and days for all those years. Inside was a heavy weight that had to be pulled to the top regularly to keep it running.

"Too bad," thought a new owner, "that such an old clock should have to bear so heavy a load." So he took the cumbersome weight off its chain and set it on the hearth. Immediately, of course, the old timepiece stopped running.

"Why did you take away my weight?" asked the clock.

"I only wanted to lighten your burden," replied the man.

"Please," said the clock, "put it back. That's what keeps me going."

From the Bible

What has happened to me has actually resulted in the advancement of the gospel, so that it has become known throughout the whole imperial guard, and to everyone else, that my imprisonment is for Christ. Most of the brothers in the Lord have gained confidence from my imprisonment and dare even more to speak the message fearlessly.

PHILIPPIANS 1:12-14

A friend of mine left his wife and two daughters recently. He said he was tired of all the demands––mortgage, school, difficult relationships. He had convinced himself that things were going to get better with all the "weight" off.

Perhaps all of us overextend ourselves at times. There is a point of physical and emotional exhaustion beyond which one simply cannot function. That's why reasonable work loads with periodic breaks for renewal are necessary for everyone. We would all be wiser to take the view of life the old preacher had. A woman called his office on Thursday––

his regular day off—and was angry that she couldn't reach him. On Sunday she gave him a piece of her mind and ended by saying, "The devil never takes a day off!" The mature Christian replied, "You're correct. And if I didn't, I'd be just like him."

Don't resent your responsibilities or perform them with sighs and complaints. They're meant to keep you going, not wear you down. They allow you to make a contribution to your world. They link you with other people. They give you the chance to make a difference in the lives of those closest to you. If this sounds too idealistic for your everyday routine, read these lines that an apostle wrote to people who lived in slavery:

"Don't just do what you have to do to get by, but work heartily, as Christ's servants doing what God wants you to do. And work with a smile on your face, always keeping in mind that no matter who happens to be giving the orders, you're really serving God" (Ephesians 6:5-7, The Message).

Starting Right Now:
Find a handful of up-sides to the list of burdens you're bearing today. God has allowed them on purpose.

_____
_____
_____
_____
_____
_____
_____
_____
_____
_____
_____
_____
_____
_____
_____
_____
_____
_____
_____
_____
_____

ADD BY SUBTRACTING

You didn't get into this craziness and chaos in a day. But you can start working your way back out of it—slowly, diligently, deliberately. Today.

SOMETHING TO START WITH

You read a lot these days about stress reduction. True enough, the pace of modern life is hectic. And most of us could use some practical tips about how to simplify our lives. But where to start? There are so many things already fixed in your list of commitments. Like me, you've probably gotten used to a schedule that is always too full and would suffer a sense of withdrawal––if not a lack of self-worth––if you cut back radically.

So perhaps the best idea is not to alter your lifestyle radically. How about just cutting back in a few sensible ways? Instead of closing your business and moving to a cabin in the mountains, just give yourself a little extra breathing space for living. As the value of simplification sinks in, you'll discover things in your routine that don't have to be there––and that stress you needlessly.

From the Bible

We encourage you, brothers, to do so even more, to seek to lead a quiet life, to mind your own business, and to work with your own hands, as we commanded you, so that you may walk properly in the presence of outsiders and not be dependent on anyone.

1 THESSALONIANS 4:10-12

Here are a few typical suggestions experts make about simplifying life:

• Go to your closet one day this week, take out ten items you haven't worn in a year, and give the items to a thrift store or church that distributes clothing to the poor. Have your spouse and children do the same thing.

• Pick a day next week and do the same thing in your kitchen. Next week go to the garage. Next week, your attic. Keep getting rid of stuff until you clear out the clutter you gripe about so frequently.

• Don't take any work home from your office or workplace today.

• As soon as you get home tonight, go directly to your phone, unplug it or turn off the ringer, and leave it off for the entire evening. Do the same thing at least one night per week for the next three months.

• The next time someone makes a request for a new commitment of time from your life, smile and say, "No, I won't be able to do that." No explanation or apology is necessary. If you can't learn to say no, your life is always going to be too chaotic.

If you've ever thought your closet, schedule, or life in general has become too cluttered, now is the time to begin making some changes. So ask yourself a couple of questions:

(1) What are the top three priorities for my life?

(2) Does my use of time reflect it?

If your priorities are constantly getting lost in the daily grind, take a step toward simplifying things. Today is a good day to begin.

Starting Right Now:
If you've read this far, you know what to do today. Slow down. Make a plan. Get your life under control.

_____

_____

_____

_____

_____

_____

_____

_____

_____

_____

_____

_____

_____

_____

_____

_____

_____

_____

_____

_____

_____

_____

THANK-YOU NOTE

If you found in your mailbox a cell phone bill, a credit card application, and a handwritten note from an old friend, which would you read first?

SOMETHING TO START WITH

Charles Fackler served his country long before war was waged with long-range missiles and smart bombs. He was an American doughboy who fought with distinction in World War I––on the ground, looking directly into the enemies' faces. He was wounded both by bullets and shrapnel, and was gassed more than once. Yet he continued to slog through the fields and forests of France.

"It was called the Bucket of Blood," recalled Fackler of the Meuse-Argonne offensive of September 1918. "We survived like animals in the tall grass, weeds, bushes, and the like. My chest looks like a checkerboard with scars."

From the Bible

I give thanks to my God for every remembrance of you, always praying with joy for all of you in my every prayer, because of your partnership in the gospel from the first day until now....

It is right for me to think this way about all of you, because I have you in my heart, and you are all partners with me in grace.

PHILIPPIANS 1:3-5,7

He was proud to have been awarded the Purple Heart. According to his pastor, it signified that he had been "wounded in the service of his country, trying to repel an aggressor and safeguard peace."

In 1988, despite the fact that most World War I veterans were dead, France decided to honor all the Allied soldiers who fought in their country's borders. On the 80th anniversary of the armistice, it was resolved that Fackler would receive the Legion of Honor medal––France's most distinguished award. But not every citation could be conferred during the anniversary year. These things simply take some time.

On January 21, 1999, everything was in place for a 2:00 p.m. presentation ceremony in Allentown, Pennsylvania. Fackler's son was there. Members of American Legion Post 576 and Veterans of Foreign Wars Post 13 came. Friends from Allentown who loved the 98-year-old man showed up. The French consul was even en route from Washington, D.C. What an afternoon it was going to be!

Then, just a few minutes before noon, Charles Fackler died from the devastation cancer had wrought in his frail body. Too late now to call off the medal ceremony, it was quickly converted into a memorial service.

All of us have people in our lives who deserve thanks and recognition. No medal, perhaps, but words spoken directly and sincerely to tell that person what he or she means to us. A thoughtfully drafted letter letting him know the difference he made. A card with a personal note inside to tell her that her effort mattered.

You've probably told others how important these people are to you. While you still can, tell them as well.

Starting Right Now:
Think of someone you could write today with a personal thanks. Start your letter something like this:

_____
_____
_____
_____
_____
_____
_____
_____
_____
_____
_____
_____
_____
_____
_____
_____
_____
_____
_____
_____
_____
_____

BITE YOUR TONGUE

If you've had a bad language habit in the past, it can be a hard thing to overcome. But do it. It doesn't speak well of you—or of the God you serve.

SOMETHING TO START WITH

Words that used to be associated with barrooms and barracks have become chic in public. Some say the Vietnam War era brought profanity into the public arena and made it acceptable. Others say the AIDS crisis put graphic sexual expressions into the public vocabulary. Wherever it came from, books and magazines splatter cuss-words freely on their pages.

We've come a long way since Clark Gable's single four-letter word made moviegoers gasp at the end of "Gone With the Wind." These days Eddie Murphy's out-of-control tongue bristles with 214 instances of the F-word in one of his latest taped performances.

And I don't like it one bit.

Profane and obscene language, off-color stories, racial slurs, swearing, and the like are offensive to God—and to morally sensitive people.

It reminds me of the old story about the devout church-going woman who bought a talking parrot. As soon as she got it home, she put her face close to the bird cage and said, "Polly want a cracker?" The bird responded with a barrage of profanity. She opened the cage, grabbed the bird by its neck, and said, "Don't you ever use language like that in my house again!" With that, she put the bird in her

From the Bible

Every creature—animal or bird, reptile or fish—is tamed and has been tamed by man, but no man can tame the tongue. It is a restless evil, full of deadly poison. With it we bless our Lord and Father, and with it we curse men who are made in God's likeness. Out of the same mouth come blessing and cursing. My brothers, these things should not be this way.

JAMES 3:7-10

kitchen freezer. Forty-five minutes later, she pulled the parrot out and asked if he had learned his lesson. The bird promised he would never again use such language. "But I do have one question," he said with a shiver. "What did the chicken do?"

Even if the threat of being turned into a frozen chicken would work to change a parrot's salty vocabulary, I don't know what it will take to effect a wholesale cultural change for the better. I can only pledge to be careful with my own mouth and encourage other believers to bridle their tongues as well.

Few things are more shocking for their sheer inconsistency than to hear a Christian's tongue gone berserk––when a woman loses her temper and begins to curse, when a man decides to make his statement emphatic by punctuating it with profanity.

I like what Peanuts cartoonist Charles Schultz said on this point: "I have a strong dislike for vulgar phrases, and I find that the terms 'good grief' and 'rats' will cover virtually anything that happens."

Starting Right Now:
You can't avoid hearing crude talk altogether, but how can you cut down on some of your exposure?

THE JOKE'S ON WHO?

You can't help but laugh at some of the foibles and inconsistencies in people's lives—until the phony becomes the same person who uses your toothbrush.

SOMETHING TO START WITH

The dictionary defines *oxymoron* as "a rhetorical figure in which incongruous or contradictory terms are joined." The English word is formed from two Greek terms—*oxus*, meaning "sharp," and *moros*, meaning "dull." It therefore identifies expressions that appear to link opposite and incompatible ideas. Common examples might be "computer reliability" or "temporary tax increase." Got the picture?

Someone recently shared a list of the "Top 50 Oxymorons" with me. Here are the ones I selected as my favorite dozen:

- *Act Naturally* • *Almost Exactly*
- *Alone Together* • *New Classic*
- *Childproof* • *Clearly Misunderstood*
- *Plastic Glasses* • *Terribly Pleased*
- *Definite Maybe* • *Pretty Ugly*
- *Rap Music* • *"Now, then…"*

The fun intended by pointing to these common terms with questionable propriety set me to thinking about more serious issues. For example, you probably have some skepticism about "unemployed workers." If they're really willing to work, there's little excuse for people to be unemployed. On the other hand, I'd hope nobody points to your company—or to you—and offers "business ethics" as an oxymoron.

From the Bible

Be doers of the word and not hearers only, deceiving yourselves. Because if anyone is a hearer of the word and not a doer, he is like a man looking at his own face in a mirror; for he looks at himself, goes away, and right away forgets what kind of man he was. But the one who looks intently into the perfect law of freedom and perseveres in it… will be blessed in what he does.

JAMES 1:22-25

What about your family? Are you an "unloving mate"? Ever take a "working vacation" with the people who want, need, and deserve your attention? The ultimate inconsistency in the life profile of any mother or father would be for someone to appropriately tag her or him with the label "absentee parent." You may be one or the other, but you're not both! Just ask your children.

Then comes your relationship with God. Ever hear what amounts to the ultimate oxymoron––"spiritual indifference"? According to Jesus, the two words cancel each other out. *The Message* makes the sense of His words emphatic: "This is war, and there is no neutral ground. If you're not on my side, you're the enemy; if you're not helping, you're making things worse" (Matthew 10:30).

Ouch! Maybe there are some less-than-funny aspects to this business of inconsistency in words, behaviors, and relationships. I don't really want to be laughed at in the things that matter—that matter eternally. I'll bet you don't either.

Starting Right Now:
Spotted some pockets of inconsistency in your life? Do the painfully powerful work of weeding them out.

SOMEBODY, SOMEWHERE

Cruel words are hard to receive without taking them personally. But try looking beyond the digs and put-downs—and see the speaker personally.

Madalyn Murray O'Hair was involved in a lawsuit upon which the Supreme Court based its 1963 decision to prohibit public schools from initiating classroom prayer. For her role in that case, she acquired the title "America's Most Hated Woman."

She founded a group called American Atheists and played to the press. She clearly enjoyed the notoriety her anti-theistic posture brought with it. Her name came to stand for opposition to theism, prayer, and all things religious.

Ms. O'Hair disappeared in September 1995. Officials think she is probably dead and have found what appear to be her remains. But there's more to the story of this angry woman you might like to know.

From the Bible

"You don't even have a bucket, and the well is deep. So where do you get this 'living water'? You aren't greater than our father Jacob, are you?…"

Jesus said, "Everyone who drinks from this water will get thirsty again. But whoever drinks from the water that I will give him will never get thirsty again–ever!

JOHN 4:11-14

In January 1999 the Internal Revenue Service sold her personal property to pay back taxes and creditor fees. Among the items auctioned were her personal diaries. According to *Christianity Today* of March 1999, the following entry appears in at least a half-dozen entries: "Somebody, somewhere, love me."

Do you know any angry, loud, obnoxious people? Anyone who always seems determined to pick a fight? Anybody who actually glories in being disliked?

In families, some children are disruptive at home and constantly in trouble at school. There are schoolchildren who terrorize other students and taunt teachers. There are shrill, quarrelsome people in offices who make everyone's task harder. And there are church bullies who regularly get loud and divisive over insignificant things.

Know what's going on in the vast majority of these situations? A frightened, insecure person is vying for attention. People who feel unloved and miserable tend to mistake attention––even scoldings, reprimands, or firings––with validation. They'd rather be spanked than ignored, kicked out of the company than face their self-doubt.

What's the best strategy for dealing with these people? "Our Scriptures tell us that if you see your enemy hungry, go buy that person lunch, or if he's thirsty, get him a drink. Your generosity will surprise him with goodness. Don't let evil get the best of you; get the best of evil by doing good" (Romans 12:20-21, *The Message*).

It's apparently too late to help Ms. O'Hair. But does anyone else come to mind?

Starting Right Now:
Think through the godly words you're going to think to yourself next time you hear some <u>ungodly</u> ones.

_____

_____

_____

_____

_____

_____

_____

_____

_____

_____

_____

_____

_____

_____

_____

_____

_____

_____

_____

_____

_____

_____

GOING UP?

Lottery ticket and diet pill buyers beware! Anything earned easily is not worth what little price you paid for it. All true winnings go to the workers.

SOMETHING TO START WITH

Years ago a yokel and his family drove to Memphis for the first time. Lost in the big city, they stopped in front of a tall hotel building. Father and son went inside to get directions and were waiting in line at a reception desk.

Suddenly they saw the wall open for an old man with a cane. They watched in amazement as the wall closed, numbers above the opening in it grew larger, then smaller, and the doors opened again. Out came a young man in confident stride and business suit.

"Son, wait here," said the farmer. "I'm going to go get in that thing!"

From the Bible

I am the least of the apostles, unworthy to be called an apostle, because I persecuted the church of God.

But by God's grace I am what I am, and His grace toward me was not ineffective. However, I worked more than any of them, yet not I, but God's grace that was with me. Therefore, whether it is I or they, so we preach and so you have believed.

1 CORINTHIANS 15:9-11

All of us could wish change came so quickly and painlessly. I'd rather lose 20 pounds with a pill than deny myself extra helpings and begin to exercise. Many choose to saddle themselves with debt rather than buy furniture when they can afford it or save money for a better car. People resent a co-worker's success rather than applying themselves with equal commitment to their own jobs.

Perhaps this is why there is such an exorbitant amount of anger in today's world. "Road rage" and its classroom, workplace, and church equivalents are less psychological than moral issues. Petty people get mad at the good fortune of others.

Selfish persons want immediately what others got over time. Immature people want handed to them on a platter the life status others attained through discipline and sacrifice.

We laugh at the bumpkin who thought an elevator was a magic box that made old into young, stooped into sprightly, and plain into stylish. Maybe we should laugh at ourselves. Going to college doesn't make one wise. Driving an expensive automobile doesn't confer personality or refinement. Living in an exclusive neighborhood says nothing about the happiness of the people in its nicest house. And going to church doesn't necessarily indicate a truly spiritual life.

Authentic change in looks, lifestyle, and personality takes place over time. So if there is an outcome you'd like, the surest way to achieve it is to set a worthwhile goal, identify the steps necessary to attain it, and then begin taking them.

The wisdom, discipline, and understanding that come from the journey are equally as valuable as any attainment at its end.

Starting Right Now:
What have you been promising yourself you'll start doing to pursue the dream God has given you?

_____
_____
_____
_____
_____
_____
_____
_____
_____
_____
_____
_____
_____
_____
_____
_____
_____
_____
_____
_____
_____
_____

TEN POUNDS OF CATFISH

Even the humblest of us know the bewilderment of being underappreciated for what we do sometimes. Does it make you want to fight, or fight on?

SOMETHING TO START WITH

Professional athletes get traded routinely. Someone needs a center fielder, and another team has two good ones. A team seeks to shore up its pitching staff and goes player swapping. Unless the trade involves a superstar, most don't make headlines. Let me tell you about one you may have missed.

Ken Krahenbuhl was playing minor league ball for the Pacific Suns in Oxnard, California. He was having a decent season, but he wasn't about to be called up to the Big Show--player jargon for the major leagues. In late July 1998, he was traded to the Greenville (Mississippi) Bluesmen for some cash, a player to be named later, and...*ten pounds of catfish.*

From the Bible

Make your own attitude that of Christ Jesus, who, existing in the form of God, did not consider equality with God as something to be used for His own advantage. Instead He emptied Himself by assuming the form of a slave, taking on the likeness of men. And when He had come as a man in His external form, He humbled Himself by becoming obedient.

PHILIPPIANS 2:5-8

So how do you spell *insulted?* "The Suns could have gotten some players in exchange for me to help their ballclub instead of the stinking catfish, but they just don't care," Krahenbuhl said. "Traded me for catfish. Can you believe that?"

Do you have any idea how he felt when word reached him of the trade? Remember the poor grade you got on a pretty decent science project you labored over in junior high? Remember not making the high school chorus or church choir one year--knowing full well there were other voices no better than your own that were accepted?

Or perhaps the slight was even more serious: You worked hard for the company and passed up an offer to work for your competitor, only to be let go during a slow quarter. You really tried to make the relationship or marriage work but were dumped for somebody else. You tried to do the right thing in a given circumstance but were misunderstood, misrepresented, and you wound up being the goat in a situation you had tried to salvage.

How did Ken Krahenbuhl handle his slight? Tear up the old team's clubhouse? Get into a fight with his manager? Promise to get even with somebody for humiliating him? He reported to Greenville, put on his new uniform, and pitched the next night.

That's the *right* way to handle a slight. Just take care of business. Buckle down to the new situation and its challenges. Make lemonade from your lemon.

By the way, he went to the mound that Friday and pitched a perfect game for his new team. Way to go, Ken! And I hope you get to the Big Show someday.

FRENCH-FRY FAITH

If you know that sick, sinking feeling of fatigue that comes from a daily diet weak in spiritual staples, here's something challenging for you to chew on.

SOMETHING TO START WITH

The bears of Yellowstone are no longer as plentiful or visible to park visitors as they used to be––like the day I sat in an audience of about seventy-five people there and watched a bear cub amble across the side of a rocky hill no more than twenty yards behind the speaker. The man was oblivious to what was happening behind him. And the audience was equally oblivious to whatever he was trying to say!

It seems people were no longer simply seeing and photographing the bears. They had begun *feeding* them––in violation of notices posted throughout the park area. And the things they were giving the bears were quite different from their normal diet of wild berries, fish, and small animals. Cupcakes and sandwich bread simply aren't good for them.

From the Bible

Everyone who lives on milk is inexperienced with the message about righteousness, because he is an infant. But solid food is for the mature–for those whose senses have been trained to distinguish between good and evil.

Therefore, leaving the elementary message about the Messiah, let us go on to maturity.

HEBREWS 5:13–6:1

Have you ever wondered how bears survive long winters in hibernation? God created them with a marvelous mechanism for storing fat in their bodies during the warmer times of the year. Then, as they sleep through the cold months in their dens, those layers of fat burn off slowly and keep them alive until spring arrives.

But the fat buildup in bears from human junk food burns off much more quickly than the fat residue from their customary diet. Thus, during the winter months, dozens of bears would exhaust their reserves, effectively starve, and then freeze to death.

I've known some believers whose lives came unraveled because they had lived on a diet of spiritual junk food. Things like Christian music, bumper stickers, and inspirational TV can serve a good purpose. But they can also be a sweet-tasting substitute for the serious pursuit of God. If they are all you're getting, you are relying on secondhand spirituality. If you merely go to church often and take your fill, you are getting relatively empty calories compared to personal time in the Word of God, serious prayer, and conscious imitation of Christ. Malnutrition may set in. You can die!

Like you, I've been taught and encouraged by others. But their experiences with God cannot count for our own. Each of us needs the nourishment of a balanced diet from healthy spiritual sources. Occasional "treats" should not be the main course.

Christian discipleship in a fallen world is no picnic. So eat and live accordingly.

Starting Right Now:
Give up junk food living for six weeks. And check back here to report how much better you feel.

MAKE-A-DIFFERENCE DAY

When a London newspaper asked for letters about what was wrong with the world, one man wrote back: "Dear sirs, I am. Sincerely, G. K. Chesterton."

SOMETHING TO START WITH

War in the Balkans. High school shootings. Killer tornadoes. Division in churches. Do you ever feel overwhelmed with the sense that something crooked needs to be straightened? That some wrong needs righting? That there is a dragon somebody needs to slay?

More often than not, the outcome of our collective hand wringing is that we lament how much bigger the problems are than our resources––and do nothing. After all, what can one person do against problems of such immense proportions?

In Alexander Solzhenitsyn's *The First Circle*, the character who appears to speak for him is Nerzhin. At one point, Nerzhin ponders this question: "If you wanted to set the world to rights, who would you begin with––yourself or other people?"

From the Bible

During the night a vision appeared to Paul: a Macedonian man was standing and pleading with him, "Cross over to Macedonia and help us!"

After he had seen the vision, we immediately made efforts to set out for Macedonia, concluding that God had called us to evangelize them.

ACTS 16:9-10

The frustration most of us feel about solving great problems is that we have no control over the fortunes and behaviors of other people. Thus we are willing to leave the problem unsolved. At least, though, we feel pious that we are aware of it now and concerned about its effects.

But the truth is that every problem about which you have a justifiable concern is one where you can begin with yourself to make a difference.

• Concerned about the war in Yugoslavia? Pray for a just peace, and encourage your church to help the refugees whose faces haunt you from the evening news.

• Worried about angry and alienated kids? Build bridges of communication and love with your own children. Or stick your neck out to share the pain of a fellow parent and support him or her through a crisis with a troubled child.

• Horrified over scenes of weather devastation? Send a personal or company donation to a reputable Christian agency helping provide emergency aid to victims.

• Grieved over division in the body of Christ? Call a brother or sister from whom you are alienated, and get together to talk and pray about the matter. Or buy lunch for two who are at odds, and try to be a third-party peacemaker for them.

Problems that remain someone else's responsibility stay unsolved forever. At some point, someone has to begin taking positive steps to make things better.

If something you know needs fixing, perhaps you can be the point of beginning.

Starting Right Now:
Is God laying something heavy on your heart? What might He want you to do about it?

DOUBLE NEGATIVES

When you pride yourself on how clean your record is, you open yourself up to a haughty layer of sins that seemed to irritate Jesus more than the others.

SOMETHING TO START WITH

A man charged with destroying a bar in a drunken brawl appeared in court. "Sir," said the judge, "what do you have to say for yourself?"

The man looked at the robed figure behind the imposing bench and said, "Your honor, I'm not guilty. My reputation in this community is spotless."

"Do you have any witnesses who can vouch for your character?" asked the judge. The man pointed across the courtroom. "The sheriff over there."

The sheriff immediately stood to his feet and said, "Your honor, that man's a liar. I've never seen him before in my life."

The man turned to the judge with a smile. "See! I've lived in this town for fifteen years, and the sheriff doesn't even know me. Isn't that character enough?"

It would seem that far too many subscribe to the mistaken idea that good character is defined by the things we *don't* do: we don't destroy bars in brawls, don't steal, don't have a criminal record, don't beat children, don't do this or that.

Good character is a collection of positive qualities committed to habit, cultivated over time and with conscious intent. They don't happen naturally, for they often go against the grain of self-interest.

From the Bible

While He was reclining at the table in the house, many tax collectors and sinners came as guests with Jesus and His disciples. When the Pharisees saw this, they asked His disciples, "Why does your Teacher eat with tax collectors and sinners?"

But when He heard this, He said, "Those who are well don't need a doctor, but the sick do. Go and learn what this means: 'I desire mercy and not sacrifice.' For I didn't come to call the righteous, but sinners."

MATTHEW 9:10-13

Yes, their presence in one's life keeps her or him from negative things such as drunken brawling or stealing. But it's hardly enough to say "I don't steal from others." Is there some suffering or helpless person for whom you care enough to help? Have you learned to give things away without begrudging them? Can you hold your success or prosperity in a loose grasp? How generous and helpful are you? How willing have you been to encourage and mentor others? Have you learned to applaud their successes without envy or resentment?

Whenever you are trying to figure out the right thing to do in a given situation, the Golden Rule remains the most straightforward principle to follow. "Here is a simple, rule-of-thumb guide for behavior: Ask yourself what you want people to do for you, then grab the initiative and do it for them. Add up God's Law and Prophets and this is what you get" (Matthew 7:12, *The Message*).

Your calling on Earth is not to curse the darkness but to reflect God's light.

Starting Right Now:
The sin in your life is worth standing against. But what do you want to be caught standing _for_?

A CIRCLE OF SUFFERING

God has put us in the Body for a reason, so that hands can dry weeping eyes, arms can embrace heavy shoulders, words can comfort weary hearts.

A woman's happiness was shattered by the loss of her brother, a good man whom she loved dearly. Distraught by her grief, she kept asking God "Why?" But hearing only silence in response to her plea, she set out to search for an answer.

She had not gone far when she came upon an old man sitting on a bench. He was weeping. "I have suffered a great loss," he said. "I am a painter and have lost my sight." He was asking the same question as the woman. "Why?" he cried. "Why me?"

Soon they overtook a young man walking aimlessly. He had lost his wife and his little girl. They had been the joys of his life, but his wife had left him for another man and had taken their daughter with her. He joined the little group of anguished travelers.

Shortly they came up to a young woman sobbing over a grave. She had lost her child to leukemia. She too joined with them in their chorus of "Oh, God, why?"

Suddenly they came upon Jesus. Each confronted Him with the question. But Jesus gave no answer, no defense. He simply began to cry and said, "I am bearing the burden of a woman who has lost her brother, a painter who has lost his eye-

From the Bible

We who are strong have an obligation to bear the weaknesses of those without strength, and not to please ourselves. Each one of us must please his neighbor for his good, in order to build him up. For even the Messiah did not please Himself. On the contrary, as it is written, "The insults of those who insult You have fallen on Me."

ROMANS 15:1-3

sight, a man who has lost his wife's love to another man, and a woman whose baby has died."

As He spoke and continued to weep, the four moved closer and closer to Him--and to one another. He reached to embrace them, and one by one the sufferers formed a circle of hurting people.

"My dominion is the dominion of the heart," Jesus said to His cluster of people with different experiences but common pain. "I cannot prevent the pain that has come to you. I can only heal it."

"How?" asked the woman.

"By sharing it," He said.

Then He was gone. And the four? They were left standing together, holding each other, supporting each other.

God's love comes to each of us through the sharing of our stories and sufferings. It makes the difference between healthy and hopeless, victorious and vanquished. It's why Alcoholics Anonymous works and many churches don't.

God's healing may be able to reach someone through you today. Be alert!

Starting Right Now:
Never think that Christian living is just between you and God. Someone you know needs you. Who?

_____
_____
_____
_____
_____
_____
_____
_____
_____
_____
_____
_____
_____
_____
_____
_____
_____
_____
_____
_____
_____
_____

BETTER THAN I DESERVE

Knowing yourself like you do, you may wonder how God could love you.
But knowing you like He does, God can still call you His precious child.

SOMETHING TO START WITH

Ever notice how people tend to live up to the labels we put on them? I watched in anguish the other day as a man scolded his little boy in the aisle of a store. "You're just a rotten little monster!" he said for several of us to hear.

The kid was being a terror, all right. But his father was making things much worse by giving the boy a negative self-image to fulfill. The embarrassed young dad who clearly didn't know what to do with his rowdy four or five-year-old was, I feared, programming the child for some unsuspecting teacher's class––or some warden's prison.

The good news from this is that it works positively as well as negatively. Maybe you've seen the musical *Man of Lamancha.* It is the story of Don Quixote, a nutty character who jousts with windmills and thinks he is a knight battling dragons. The most poignant part of the musical is his relationship with Aldonza.

Aldonza was a worthless slut, the town whore, a hopeless piece of human trash. But to Don Quixote, she was "Dulcinea"––a name that means "Sweet One." The townspeople would howl with

From the Bible

Look at how great a love the Father has given us, that we should be called God's children. And we are! The reason the world does not know us is that it didn't know Him.

Dear friends, we are God's children now, and what we will be has not yet been revealed. We know that when He appears, we will be like Him, because we will see Him as He is.

And everyone who has this hope in Him purifies himself just as He is pure.

1 JOHN 3:1-3

laughter when the crazy knight called her by so tender and flattering a name. Yet he never relented. To him, she was Dulcinea. He loved her with a pure love that was unlike any she had ever experienced. He refused to see her as others did.

Near the end of the musical, Don Quixote is dying, and Aldonza is with him. When he has taken his last breath, she begins to sing "The Impossible Dream." It is an inspiring song that dares the human spirit to dream, to soar, to achieve. As the last note of the song fades away, someone shouts, "Aldonza!" But the woman stands up defiantly, responding, "My name is Dulcinea!" She had been transformed by the kindness of a would-be knight. A woman without self-respect had come to believe that she was a lady who deserved to be treated with dignity.

If life has labeled you unflatter-ingly, God's voice can still be heard above the chaotic noise. Hold that thought as you take on another day in the strength of God's empowering love.

Starting Right Now:
As a believer in Christ, God has declared you pure and holy in His sight. How does that make you feel?

_____
_____
_____
_____
_____
_____
_____
_____
_____
_____
_____
_____
_____
_____
_____
_____
_____
_____
_____
_____
_____
_____
_____

THE MAGIC BELT

The hazards of life that have tripped up others won't be able to work on you, you think, because you've got something others don't have. Or do you?

SOMETHING TO START WITH

Colonel Pascal Gbah of the Ivory Coast Army was fatally wounded August 26, 1998, while testing a piece of equipment––a "magic belt" that was supposed to protect him from bullets. Andre Gondo, the colonel's cousin who made the belt and whose 20-year-old son fired the test bullet, was still insisting that its protective powers were real after being taken into custody over the incident.

My first reaction to this story was simple, straightforward horror. How could anyone believe a "magic belt" would protect him from bullets? Next I was tempted to laugh out loud at the lunacy of the scenario. But that was quickly suppressed as I thought about how much like Colonel Gbah we all can be.

From the Bible

Timothy, my child, I am giving you this instruction in keeping with the prophecies previously made about you, so that by them you may strongly engage in battle, having faith and a good conscience.

Some have rejected these and have suffered the shipwreck of their faith.

1 TIMOTHY 1:18-19

• The high school jock believes his ability to advance a football will be his "magic belt." So he doesn't worry about English, math, and history. When he gets a scholarship offer from a major university, he can't qualify academically. What he thought would carry him through wasn't enough to get him to a competitive level.

• The university co-ed thinks her ability to turn heads when she walks into a room filled with males is more important than completing her education. So she drops out, makes a little money, and gets a couple of promotions on her sales staff.

After three years, she wonders why "things just aren't working out" in her life. Turning a few heads with youthful beauty was too insecure a foundation for building an adult life.

• Perhaps these two individuals get their educational priorities straight and stay in college. Graduation leads to professional school. Competition exhilarates and brings out the best. Then come marriage, a couple of children, even occasional church attendance. But after a major crisis, both marriage and career collapse. The "magic belt" of church membership wasn't enough to survive a challenge that required personal faith and an authentic relationship with God.

History is littered with the corpses of those who let luck or wishful thinking stand where personal faith, wise choices, and solid character belong.

"My child, hold on to wisdom and reason. Don't let them out of your sight. They will give you life. Like a necklace, they will beautify your life" (Proverbs 3:21-22, New Century Version).

Starting Right Now:
What "magic belt" have you tried wearing before? And how much different has life been without it?

HAPPY FEET

Sometimes it only takes the smallest change or kindness to make a big difference in the lives of our employees, our friends, and our families.

SOMETHING TO START WITH

A little-heralded change is making a major difference in the United States Marine Corps. No, the Marines aren't getting new-fangled rifles, communications satellites, or ground-to-air missiles.

They're getting new boots.

The traditional method of procuring footgear for the U.S. military involved a bureaucrat delivering a tome of government-written specifications to shoe companies about how to build boots. Not only were the particulars stated in obtuse language, but they were also terribly outdated.

The president of one manufacturing company finally had the courage to tell the military: "You guys are stuck back in the 1940s when it comes to shoe technology." Millions of dollars of research that had gone into the civilian market was being overlooked. Soldiers were still being issued combat boots that were essentially unchanged since World War II.

A study by the Navy and Johns Hopkins University found that lower-extremity injuries such as shin-splints and stress fractures were the primary cause of recruits washing out of boot camp. But a traditionalist mentality held that boots good enough for fighting men in Europe and Vietnam were good enough for today's soldiers.

From the Bible

Esteem them very highly in love because of their work. Be at peace among yourselves. And we exhort you, brothers: warn those who are lazy, comfort the discouraged, help the weak, be patient with everyone. See to it that no one repays evil for evil to anyone, but always pursue what is good for one another and for all.

1 THESSALONIANS 5:13-15

In November 1997, however, the Marine Corps began issuing new boots to its inductees. Originally designed for civilian hikers and outdoor enthusiasts, they are lighter, cooler, more shock-absorbing, and more water-resistant than the old model. The soles have better grip, and their linings are softer and more fungus-resistant. They have drastically reduced foot problems while elevating morale.

Could your workplace benefit from fresh thinking about repetitive tasks or recalcitrant problems? Outdated procedures of inventory control, accounting, and communication tend to be more expensive and less efficient. And insisting on staying with them often undermines morale. Three hundred dollars worth of fresh paint on interior walls might do more for everyone in the office than a $90,000 refurbishing of its exterior.

Comfortable boots for a soldier, a decent chair for a secretary, clean restrooms for customers—the "little things" sometimes do more than major overhauls to raise both sales and spirits.

IS EVERYBODY HAPPY?

We feel better when we get everyone's approval and consensus, but we could save ourselves a lot of needless posturing if we were satisfied with God's O.K.

SOMETHING TO START WITH

Have you ever gotten caught in the trap of trying to please everybody?

Why, even *God* can't please everybody. The farmer is praying for rain on his fields the same day a Scout leader is praying it won't rain out a camping trip. You autumn enthusiasts are praying for extended periods of fall color while those of us with debilitating allergies can't wait for the first couple of killing frosts. The elderly man who hopes for a mild winter without heavy snows because of his heart condition is counterbalanced by a fifth grader who prays for snow so he can miss school. If God Himself can't please everybody, should it surprise us that we can't? Only a fool thinks he or she can do what is beyond God!

So whom should you try to please? Family members who want more of your time or a boss who wants more hours at the office or on the road? Your company's shareholders or your clients? Your quota or your conscience?

Maybe we should all take our cue on this one from Jesus. He kept His life in balance by honoring one supreme obligation, one highest overseer. His one boss was God. He had an audience of One and was dedicated to pleasing Him above all else--and all others.

From the Bible

"I can do nothing on My own. Only as I hear do I judge, and My judgment is righteous, because I do not seek My own will, but the will of Him who sent Me.

"If I testify about Myself, My testimony is not valid. There is Another who testifies about Me, and I know that the testimony He gives about Me is valid."

JOHN 5:30-32

• If the first question you ask is, "What does God want of me in this situation?" then your focus has been automatically centered.

• If you commit to doing the right thing above the pressing or politically correct thing, you have defined your moral duty to be more critical than any competing selfish interest.

• If you do what God wants you to do, it will always be right to do *that*––no matter what anyone else thinks of it.

I know full well that this rule of thumb doesn't settle every hard case. But it sets the right tone for a life well-lived. It solves more cases than we might want to admit. And it frees you of an overwhelming need for the approval of others that can dominate and destroy your life. Jesus was never stressed out over the fear of rejection, for He always knew He was serving an audience of One.

In the end, it is only God you want to hear say, "Well done!" His opinion is the only one that matters. Are you clear about whose approval you will seek today?

SEEK AND YE SHALL FIND

We can find fault with just about everybody we know—and break down relationships that God intended to use for purposes bigger than our pettiness.

SOMETHING TO START WITH

A knight traveling to a great city was nearing its gates when he asked an old man seated beside the road, "What are the people like in the city ahead?"

"What were they like in your own city?" the man replied.

"They were a terrible lot," the knight declared. "Mean, untrustworthy, detestable in every respect––there was not a man or woman in that terrible place I could trust."

"Aha!" said the old man. "You will find them the same in the city before you."

No more had the first knight ridden off than another stopped to ask the same question to the same old man. Again, the old man replied by inquiring about the people the knight had known in his city of origin. The knight received the question with a sigh and wistful look.

"They were fine people all," he proclaimed. "They were so honest and hardworking, so selfless and kindhearted that I was sad beyond words to leave."

"And just such people as you have described will you find in the city that lies ahead of you," said the wise man who sat just outside its gates.

From the Bible

You, why do you criticize your brother? Or you, why do you look down on your brother? For we will all stand before the judgment seat of God. For it is written: "As I live, says the Lord, every knee will bow to Me, and every tongue will give praise to God." So then, each of us will give an account of himself to God.

Therefore, let us no longer criticize one another, but instead decide not to put a stumbling block or pitfall in your brother's way.

ROMANS 14:10-13

You and I know why this story has survived. It tells a fundamental truth about human nature. One tends to find in his new city or new company, new friends or new employer, new church or new mate the same thing he saw in the one just left.

If anyone applies for a job in your workplace and spends the interview time telling you how sorry his last boss was or how unhappy she is in her present situation, try to find someone else to hire. Even if that person goes out of his way to flatter you or to say wonderful things about your company, you can count on getting the very same reviews for yourself and your firm within six months.

Preachers who have any sense at all hope the family that left the church three blocks away because they didn't like the preacher will go to any church in town besides their own! Whatever they didn't like there, they'll soon come to hate here.

Your expectations of others generally dictate what you find in them. So be careful what you go looking to see in them today.

ELEMENTARY, MY DEAR

In a culture growing more cynical and secular by the hour, we must work harder than ever to make sure our beliefs are grounded in biblical bedrock.

SOMETHING TO START WITH

Sherlock Holmes and Dr. Watson were on a camping trip. They had retired early but had both awakened around 2 a.m. With a clear, star-studded night sky above them, Holmes asked, "Watson, what do you see?"

"Well," said the doctor, "I see thousands of stars!"

"And what does that mean to you?" pressed the detective.

"I suppose it means that we are most fortunate to inhabit God's great universe as intelligent observers. Although we are small in His eyes, we are blessed with powers of reasoning that permit us to make our way in this world of blind greed and criminal enterprises. And surely a night so clear and beautiful as this is a portent of another beautiful day for us to enjoy tomorrow, dear friend. What does it mean to you, Holmes?"

"To me, Watson, it means that––while we were sleeping––someone has stolen our tent!"

Similarly, while we fortunate people reflect on our educational, scientific, and technological achievements, we may be overlooking the fact that something has been taken from us––things like innocence, propriety, and decency.

The tent of *objective moral norms* by which to frame and judge human conduct

From the Bible

Evil people and imposters will become worse, deceiving and being deceived. But as for you, continue in what you have learned and firmly believed, knowing those from whom you learned, and that from childhood you have known the sacred Scriptures, which are able to instruct you for salvation through faith in Christ Jesus.

2 TIMOTHY 3:13-15

has been stolen from this generation. Not only the tent, but the pegs of objective truth necessary to hold it in place have been ripped from the ground. Indeed, if you press today's thought leaders (i.e., spin doctors), you will hear them explain in condescending tones that there is no "real" ground of history and meaning beneath our feet. There is only the ongoing process of interpretation, no definite or fixed meaning to anything.

In a commencement speech at Stanford University on June 14, 1998, Ted Koppel counseled graduates: "Aspire to decency. Practice civility toward one another. Admire and emulate ethical behavior wherever you find it. Apply a rigid standard of morality to your lives; and if, periodically, you fail--as you surely will--adjust your lives, not the standards." That's good advice for people of all ages and backgrounds.

Before we speculate on the meaning of the stars, Dr. Watson, we must pay attention to finding the tent that has disappeared. We need to put it back in place.

Starting Right Now:
Unpopular as it may be, there are things to stand for and things to stand against. Name some:

_____
_____
_____
_____
_____
_____
_____
_____
_____
_____
_____
_____
_____
_____
_____
_____
_____
_____
_____
_____
_____
_____

GOD IN SECOND GRADE

If you haven't been finding God in the routine whereabouts of your daily life, it's not because He isn't there. You just haven't been looking very hard.

SOMETHING TO START WITH

Jan and Megan were driving home at night recently, when eight-year-old Megan asked her mother to turn the radio up. Jan ventured they could do without the noise of the radio and suggested that her little girl use the quiet time to pray.

Driving on through the undisturbed darkness, Jan eventually noticed that Megan was waving out the window. Since the sunlight was long gone, she asked what she was doing. "I'm waving at God!" came the reply. "You know, Mom, God is always with me."

From the Bible

Martha, the dead man's sister, told Him, "Lord, he already stinks. It's been four days."

Jesus said to her, "Did I not tell you that if you believed you would see the glory of God?"...

Then Jesus raised His eyes and said, "Father, I thank You that You heard Me. I know that You always hear Me, but because of the crowd standing here I said this, so they may believe You sent Me."

JOHN 11:39-42

"And you know," her daughter concluded, "God goes to second grade too."

Of course, He does. God goes to second grade, flies on airplanes, sits in on your family dinner conversations, and goes to work with you every day. The point of calling this fact to mind is not to scare you or warn you to watch your language during coffee break. Instead, I mean to encourage you to feel secure in all those places, to remind you that you are not on your own out there, to foster the sense in you that Megan enjoys about the easy and unpretentious nature of prayer.

I believe God saw Megan wave at Him in that dark night. I further believe that He took great pleasure in her guileless and innocent gesture. Would that all of us could be so conscious of God that we are constantly engaged in mental conversation with Him. Would that we felt such a continual yearning for Him that we could have no experience apart from a keen sensibility of His presence in it. Would that we understood that prayer is more than eyes closed and head bowed.

Think about your own work environment for a moment. Ever wish you could trade it for a climate more favorable to pure speech, ethical behavior, and positive relationships? Instead of looking for another job, take another view of the one you have already. Realize that God sells widgets, supervises inventory, and takes customer complaints.

If Megan senses God in the darkness, waves to Him in prayer, and knows He attends second grade with her, maybe it is not beyond us to know that He is going to be with us in every circumstance of this day—and for us to be reassured by that thought.

Starting Right Now:
Here's a good way to start the conversation today: "I know You're here, God. I love You. I'm listening."

THE PEACE CHILD

Sharing the gospel of Jesus Christ successfully with other people does not require a formula or method but a heart open to God's will and His ways.

SOMETHING TO START WITH

Don and Carol Richardson worked as missionaries among the Sawi people of Indonesia. When they went to these isolated, head-hunting cannibals in the early 1960s, they struggled to learn enough of their language to share the gospel. Finally Don climbed the ladder into the Sawi man-house and, surrounded by the skulls of cannibalized victims, began trying to teach in the terms and categories familiar to him. The Sawi were bored and unresponsive.

From the Bible

Some said, "What is this pseudo-intellectual trying to say?" Others replied, "He seems to be a preacher of foreign deities."...

Then Paul stood in the middle of the Areopagus and said, "Men of Athens! I see that you are extremely religious in every respect. For as I was passing through and observing the objects of your worship, I even found an altar on which was inscribed: "To an Unknown God." Therefore, what you worship in ignorance, this I proclaim to you."

ACTS 17:18,22-23

Fear and frustration at last led the missionaries to leave. But when tribal leaders learned of their plan, they said, "If you will stay, we promise to make peace in the morning."

The very next day, Don and Carol witnessed an incredible ceremony. Two hostile groups were positioned opposite their house on either side of a clearing. A tangible suspense wafted in the air. Finally, a man picked up his newborn child and dashed across the meadow. His wife ran after him, screaming and begging for her baby to be given back to her. Unable to catch him, she fell to her knees on the ground and sobbed for her infant.

The child's father presented his baby to the enemy clan. "Plead the peace child for me," he said. "I give you my son, and I give you my name." Soon thereafter, someone from the recipient tribe performed the same agonizing ritual in reverse. And for as long as those peace children remained alive (Don was later told), the two warring factions were bound to each other in peace.

Suddenly, Don realized he had his analogy of redemption! He climbed into the Sawi man-house again to tell the story of the ultimate Peace Child given to humankind by the one true God. Chiefs who had been unresponsive to the gospel sat spellbound. Over time, he continued to develop a theology based on Jesus, the Peace Child.

A few and finally hundreds of the once-warring, once-cannibalistic souls received Christ, until large groups of new believers were gathering for worship.

There are signs and symbols all around you that will unlock the Good News for others—if you'll ask God to show them to you.

PICKING OUT PALLBEARERS

In a world that's learned how to drive-thru and pay-at-the-pump, you almost get to thinking you can get along just fine by yourself, thank you.

SOMETHING TO START WITH

No, I haven't received a terminal diagnosis--other than life. And I have no scientific reason to think my death is imminent--though who knows if I will die before this book gets read by anyone? These are not the things that have me contemplating pallbearers today, but rather an offhand comment made by an acquaintance of mine.

"I've really had my priorities all screwed up for the past several years," he said. "I've worked hard and made a lot of money. My family life is in pretty good shape. But I've cut myself off from so many people who wanted to be my friends. Now it has dawned on me that I have scores of *acquaintances* but hardly any bona fide *friends.* I'm not even sure I could name enough people to be pallbearers at my funeral who could say we were really friends. I wonder if it's too late to change that?"

His comment wasn't made in a tone of self-pity. It was a simple acknowledgment of fact. It was also something of a confession. And it was on-target too.

Now, try this little thought experiment:

• *Name six people who are close enough friends that you would be willing to trust them with your deepest, darkest secret.*

From the Bible

Saul grew more capable, and kept confounding the Jews who lived in Damascus by proving that this One is the Messiah.

After many days had passed, the Jews conspired to kill him, but their plot became known to Saul. So they were watching the gates day and night intending to kill him, but his disciples took him by night and lowered him in a large basket through an opening in the wall.

ACTS 9:22-25

They must be people you would spontaneously think to call about a serious problem in your business, professional, family, or personal life. They must be persons from whom you would hide nothing. If you have such people in your life, their names should come to mind quickly and easily.

If you have any doubt that the people you named are really your friends, ask yourself the question in reverse:

• *Do these people trust me with their deepest, darkest secrets?*

Have they turned to you for compassion, encouragement, and help when things were difficult in their lives? Can you see yourself being asked by their families to be pallbearers at their funerals?

People who don't value friendships won't form any. And the key to having friends really is as simple as being genuinely friendly—caring, encouraging, ready to help others in their tough times. By all means, don't play at friendship.

You'll need pallbearers someday. I hope it will be an easy task to identify them.

Starting Right Now:
Make that list of true friends. And do all you can to keep every one of those friendships close.

_____
_____
_____
_____
_____
_____
_____
_____
_____
_____
_____
_____
_____
_____
_____
_____
_____
_____
_____
_____
_____
_____
_____

DID I DO THAT?

You'll never rise above the risk of embarrassing yourself badly in public—or of receiving from Christ the grace and freedom to get up and go again.

SOMETHING TO START WITH

You know the term "blooper," don't you? You've probably seen some of these lines that are allegedly taken from church newsletters:

• Don't let worry kill you. Our church can help.

• Remember all those who are sick of our church.

• For our guests who have children and don't know it, we have an attended nursery in the education building.

• Tonight's sermon: "What Is Hell?" Come early and hear our choir practice.

• A chili supper will be held tonight in the fellowship hall. Music follows.

From the Bible

Since we have a great high priest…Jesus the Son of God—let us hold fast to the confession. For we do not have a high priest who is unable to sympathize with our weaknesses, but One who has been tested in every way as we are, yet without sin. Therefore let us approach the throne of grace with boldness, so that we may receive mercy and find grace to help us at the proper time.

HEBREWS 4:14-16

Maybe reading these gaffes reminds you of a presentation you were making one time when your garbled syntax set the house rolling––and turned your face beet red. *I'm not about to tell you my worst-ever pulpit blooper!*

But how do you handle it when you mess up? Well, it's best just to laugh at yourself along with everyone else. They've all done the same thing and will be sympathetic––even if unmerciful for a day or two. The worst thing to do is to pretend nothing happened or to deny the obvious. So blush, own up, and move on!

This same approach works best with life's more serious moments too. Chances are that you won't make it through today without messing up at something. It may be as trivial as spilling your coffee or as serious as hurting someone's feelings. You might forget an appointment, jeopardize an old friendship, or lose your temper.

I'm not minimizing any of these things. Actions have consequences, and some of the things we do have more serious, negative implications than others. No rational person sets out to sabotage her career or to make a mess of his life.

But if you have a tendency toward perfectionism, lighten up! A perfectionist has been taught (probably by parents) that he or she has to be flawless to win approval and love. Acknowledge and enjoy your successes in the little, everyday things. If the report is in good shape at midnight, don't fuss with the minutiae until 3 a.m. And since you're going to find imperfections in whatever you do, make a mental note of what will work better next time rather than trash everything you've done with the job just finished.

Every pencil comes with an eraser attached. Doesn't that tell you something?

_____
_____
_____
_____
_____
_____
_____
_____
_____
_____
_____
_____
_____
_____
_____
_____
_____
_____
_____
_____

YOUR DEFINING ROLE

One of the greatest challenges in Christian living is being able to take the praise that comes attached to your name and genuinely attach it to God.

SOMETHING TO START WITH

He always wore a mask to conceal his identity. But there was no sinister purpose behind it. He was not a thief or villain. Quite the opposite! He was a heroic figure who championed justice, fair play, and honesty. He and his "faithful Indian companion," Tonto, covered each other's backs and came to the defense of the helpless. At the end they rode away before the people they had helped could make a fuss over them.

No, he is not a character from today's crop of ambiguous, self-congratulating heroes. Those of us who watched him on TV in our childhood will never hear Rossini's "William Tell Overture" without thinking of him. We will picture him riding Silver, the "fiery horse with the speed of light" and hear the announcer say, "Return with us now to those thrilling days of yesteryear. The Lone Ranger rides again."

Clayton Moore, 85, died December 28, 1999. But his death was reported in terms of the character with whose identity he will always be associated, the Lone Ranger. He was the Western hero in 169 episodes of a popular television show that

From the Bible

Thanks be to God, who always puts us on display in Christ, and spreads through us in every place the scent of knowing Him. For to God we are the fragrance of Christ among those who are being saved and among those who are perishing. To some we are a scent of death leading to death, but to others, a scent of life leading to life. And who is competent for this? For we are not like the many who make a trade in God's message for profit, but as those with sincerity, we speak in Christ, as from God and before God.

2 CORINTHIANS 2:14-17

ran from 1949 to 1957 and in two Hollywood movies. When TV and movies no longer wanted him for the role, he simply couldn't give it up. He was so closely identified with the Lone Ranger that his is the only star on the Hollywood Walk of Fame that has both his name and his character's name inscribed on it.

In reflecting on the death of one of my boyhood icons, it occurred to me that there is a parable in Clayton Moore's experience. *Once he discovered the defining role for his life, he became so marked by it that no one could ever think of him apart from it.* I'd like to be that way in relation to Jesus.

I was not born to the role, and it doesn't come naturally. It was offered by God, accepted by faith, and is lived by the power of the Spirit. But when I die, I'd like for those who notice to be as unable to report it apart from my identification with Jesus as they were to report Moore's death without mentioning his alter ego.

If you are Christ's, let His identity define yours today—and forever.

Starting Right Now:
When others give you credit for the good things you do, what could you say to deflect the praise?

NEEDS WITHIN REACH

We who are made in the image of God cannot merely notice the world's problems—we feel compelled to do something. But what? And how?

SOMETHING TO START WITH

Many of us dream of being involved in something that will change the world. So one person becomes active in politics, another in education, and still another in a business or profession that stands to affect the masses. But deep down we wonder if anyone can really make a difference?

The first atomic bomb used in war was dropped over Hiroshima, Japan, in 1945. Dr. Fumio Shigeto was waiting for a streetcar about a mile from the center of the blast. He was sheltered from its deadly force by the corner of a concrete building. Stunned and disoriented by an explosive force more devastating than anything humankind had ever experienced, he had no idea what had happened.

Dr. Shigeto's bewilderment quickly turned into a sense of overwhelming inadequacy. He was one physician with a tiny black bag still in his hand. Yet all around him he could hear the screams of desperately wounded men and women. He needed an *army* of physicians, nurses, and technicians. He needed *tons* of supplies. He needed every bed in *dozens* of hospitals. What could one man with so little at his disposal do in the face of such an incredible situation of need?

From the Bible

So many people gathered together that there was no more room, even near the door, and [Jesus] was speaking the message to them. Then they came to Him bringing a paralytic, carried by four men. Since they were not able to bring him to Jesus because of the crowd, they removed the roof where He was....

Seeing their faith, Jesus told the paralytic, "Son, your sins are forgiven."

MARK 2:2-5

He did this: The stunned survivor knelt, opened his medical bag, and began treating the person lying at his feet.

Dr. Shigeto's experience parallels our own. We look around and see such incredible devastation in our world that it is easy to be paralyzed and do nothing. After all, what difference can one person make against such formidable odds?

God doesn't expect you to change the whole world. He is not holding you accountable for helping everybody in need. That is a burden too heavy and impossible for anyone. But there is a hint of what you can and ought to do in the example of Jesus. Although He preached to huge crowds, He touched and healed people one at a time.

There is one lonely person or one frightened child you can help today. There is someone you know whose marriage is in trouble or who is about to die from her alcoholism. There is a kid failing history class or a friend at work who is depressed.

Forget about changing the world. Reach out to just one person near you today.

Starting Right Now:
Start keeping an ongoing list of people God brings to mind—people who need just a little bit of you.

TOO COOL TO GOOF UP?

You don't have to start a project with bad intentions for it to go wrong.
Sometimes the noblest of motives can lead to a monumental embarrassment.

SOMETHING TO START WITH

A group called The Bureau for At-Risk Youth of Plainview was concerned about how to communicate a clear anti-drug message to young people. So it printed thousands and thousands of pencils bearing the following slogan: "Too Cool to Do Drugs." Good idea, right? As you might have guessed, however, there is more to the story.

A ten-year-old student at Ticonderoga (New York) Elementary School caught something the adults had missed. When the pencils are sharpened a few times, the message turned into "Cool to Do Drugs." Sharpen it another time or two, and the slogan becomes an emphatic "Do Drugs." Nobody intended for that to happen! There were lots of red faces.

"We're actually a little embarrassed that we didn't notice that sooner," said a company spokeswoman. Kodi Mosier, the student who spotted the gaffe, was asked how he thought it could happen. "I guess they didn't sharpen their pencils," was his insightful response.

So the group that printed the pencils apologized and recalled them. Now they are having a new batch manufactured––

From the Bible

I myself supposed it was necessary to do many things in opposition to the name of Jesus the Nazarene. This I actually did in Jerusalem, and I locked up many of the saints in prison, since I had received authority for that from the chief priests. When they were put to death, I cast my vote against them....Since I have obtained help that comes from God, to this day I stand and testify...that the Messiah must suffer, and that as the first to rise from the dead, He would proclaim light to our people and to the Gentiles.

ACTS 26:9-10,22-23

with the same message being printed in the opposite direction. Reading now from eraser to tip instead of the opposite direction, "Too Cool to Do Drugs" will simply become "Too Cool to Do" and finally "Too Cool" as the pencils are sharpened. That's at least an improvement.

We can all say, "Been there; done that." Right? We meant well--but blew it. It was a bright idea for company morale or productivity. It was a surprise party or special gift for a family member. It was a comment in Sunday School class. Then the whole world seemed to stand on its head because of the way things backfired.

Embarrassment is best handled by a simple, straightforward acknowledgment. Getting defensive only digs your hole deeper. Looking for someone else to blame just makes you look worse. The right thing to do is to step up, take responsibility, and apologize. There is something marvelously disarming to an angry client or offended friend when you say, "I'm really very sorry about that, and I apologize. I hope you will forgive me."

Some solutions are so simple that we routinely overlook them.

Starting Right Now:
Have you done something foolish lately you've been trying to defend? Here's a nice place to repent:

_____
_____
_____
_____
_____
_____
_____
_____
_____
_____
_____
_____
_____
_____
_____
_____
_____
_____
_____
_____
_____
_____
_____

FIT FOR AN ANGEL?

There isn't a lot about the now-almost-vanished Shakers I would promote. But there is one notable exception—quality and pride of workmanship.

SOMETHING TO START WITH

In case you don't know their history, the Shakers were formed in England in the mid-1700s as an offshoot of a revival movement among the Quakers. Originally known as the "Shaking Quakers" because of the dancing and shouting that accompanied some of their rites, the group came to America and reached its peak in the 1840s. There were nearly 5,000 members in communes scattered from Maine to Kentucky.

Shakers lived as Brothers and Sisters in celibate groups. This attitude toward marriage alomg with an absence of evangelism meant the sect could not survive. Today there are believed to be only six members left.

From the Bible

Let brotherly love continue.

Don't neglect to show hospitality, for by doing this some have welcomed angels as guests without knowing it.

Remember the prisoners, as though you were in prison with them, and the mistreated, as though you yourselves were suffering bodily.

HEBREWS 13:1-3

Most people who know the Shaker movement at all know it for high-quality handicrafts rather than theology or history. For sheer elegance of style and structure, nothing quite matches their baskets, boxes, tables, wardrobes, cupboards, and chairs. The famous ladderback chair-- which came to be a Shaker symbol--was sought and prized by people in the world outside their communes. It was a staple item to a once-bustling network of commercial enterprises run by the Shakers.

When one of their craftsmen was asked how he or she built such beautiful and functional items, this was the standard answer: *"Creative work is a gift from God."* Thomas Merton, a poet and Trappist monk, once offered that the perfection of a Shaker chair came from the laborer's belief that "an angel might come and sit in it."

Wonder what it would do for everyone's task in your workplace today if such thinking dominated?

• A receptionist answers every call and greets every person through the door as if she might be speaking to an angel.

• Clerks speak to customers, tally their purchases, and make their change with the thought that this person might be a visitor from heaven.

• A nurse cares for a frail old man with the attention and tenderness befitting an angel.

• Workers on the line and sales personnel manufacture and offer products to the public in the belief that an angel just might wear this suit or eat this food, drive this car or need the protection of this insurance policy.

Take pride in what you do today. An angel just might be your next client.

GO FOR THE JUGULAR

The clothes you put on this morning are not casual dress—they are battle armor. Brace yourself for war today, and don't consider defeat as an option.

Valentin Grimaldo was walking with his brother along U.S. Highway 281 near Encino, Texas, when he reached over into some tall grass. As soon as his hand plunged into the weeds, the fangs of a deadly coral snake bit into his flesh. Lethal venom with the power to take his life quickly flowed into his body.

Quick thinking and decisive, gritty action saved his life. A spokesperson for the hospital where Mr. Grimaldo was treated said, "He grabbed the snake and bit its head off. He skinned it and used the skin as a tourniquet to keep the venom from spreading." A passerby who saw the frantic brothers stopped, put them into his car, and drove them to the hospital's emergency room.

From the Bible

Since you put away lying, "Speak the truth, each one to his neighbor," because we are members of one another.…

Don't give the Devil an opportunity. The thief must no longer steal. Instead, he must do honest work with his own hands, so that he has something to share with anyone in need.

EPHESIANS 4:25,27-28

Valentin's brother kept the snake's head as a souvenir of the harrowing adventure the two men shared.

The story reminds me of a phenomenon I've watched play itself out time and time again: *Something Satan intended to destroy a believer winds up being turned back on itself (and the devil!) and becomes a means of deliverance.*

• A business failure and bankruptcy were going to destroy a man, tear his family apart, and drive him to suicide. Now he's a financial counselor who teaches others to be prudent and responsible with money.

• Childhood abuse and heavy drug use in college had destined a woman for a path of despair that would have her destroying others as well as herself. She works with kids at a rehab center today—as part of her own recovery.

• Criminal activity, humiliation, and jail were supposed to make a young man bitter, angry, and incorrigible. He is out of prison now, working hard, and making a living for his family. He has started a prison ministry at his church.

God works with people who are willing to take decisive action against the devil's devices, not only to deliver them from his clutches but to empower those persons to use what they have learned to help others. The decisive action is called repentance; the empowerment comes via the Holy Spirit. It is God's doing.

Whatever is threatening you today, whatever joy-killer or spiritual enemy has been sent against you, God can get you out of its grasp, turn its venom back on itself, and show you how to use what you've learned to bless others.

Don't lie down beside the road and die. Be decisive. Trust His grace.

Starting Right Now:
Where has the devil been striking at you? Are you just going to sit there, or stand your ground?

_____
_____
_____
_____
_____
_____
_____
_____
_____
_____
_____
_____
_____
_____
_____
_____
_____
_____
_____
_____
_____

THE 50K NOTE

How often we sit around wondering why kids are so disrespectful these days and whatever happened to manners. Well, what's happened to ours?

SOMETHING TO START WITH

When Peter Cummings was a little boy, his mother told him how important it was to write thank-you notes. So it became second nature to him. And when he became chairman of the Detroit Symphony Orchestra in 1998, he began writing personal notes to anyone contributing $500 or more to the orchestra.

When Mary Webber Parker donated $50,000 to the orchestra, Cummings sat down and composed a note to her. Two weeks later she wrote back and promised another $50,000. Cummings wrote her again. The upshot of the exchanges was a donation of $500,000 a year for five years––a most generous $2.5 million boon to the arts in Detroit!

From the Bible

I thank God…when I constantly remember you in my prayers night and day.

Remembering your tears, I long to see you so that I may be filled with joy, clearly recalling your sincere faith that first lived in your grandmother Lois, then in your mother Eunice, and that I am convinced is in you also.

2 TIMOTHY 1:3-5

All of us who have had mothers or mentors have been taught life's "little things." But we tend to lose sight of them as we grow up, pursue our adult life goals, and focus on life's *big* things. But instead of continuing to neglect them, letting our lives grow coarser and our attitudes grumpier, let's promise to recapture our attention to the little things that collectively compose and define life.

Make it a point today to thank someone for something. Whether a person you know well or a stranger you are likely never to see again, respond to the man or woman who renders you a service, helps you with a project, or makes your world a bit more pleasant with a smile--not in hopes of getting a Peter Cummings-like reward, but simply because it is right.

Does your wife or your husband start the morning coffee? Do you work for a good boss or have a loyal assistant? Do you like the way the laundry does your shirts? Do the people who service your car do it well? Does your Sunday School teacher do a good job with the class? Then say so to that person. Or tell that person's supervisor or his or her company president about it.

Even if you do nothing more than smile and nod to someone who holds a door for you or say thanks to the postman, that moment of contact builds community. It affirms another human being. It connects two people who may never know each other's names.

There will be a reward in it for you—something more valuable than money—like making a friend or becoming a partner with God in nourishing another soul.

Starting Right Now:
Turn your drive time into a brainstorming session. Thoughtful people make thoughtfulness happen.

_____
_____
_____
_____
_____
_____
_____
_____
_____
_____
_____
_____
_____
_____
_____
_____
_____
_____
_____
_____
_____
_____

LISTEN TO YOUR HEART

It doesn't take much of an actor to fool people into believing you're someone that you're not. But it takes a real fool to make yourself believe it too.

SOMETHING TO START WITH

Practically all of us accept Jesus' proverb that a tree is known by its fruit. The point of the proverb is that a person's actions reveal to an observing world her or his innermost beliefs, commitments, and desires. Yet it is certainly possible for people to mislead others by their actions. The church has its occasional hypocrite. Marriage has its occasional gigolo. People mask their true feelings by smiling when they want to cry, giving gifts when they are basically stingy, or feigning love in order to exploit someone.

A much more reliable dictum about the heart is this one: "As water presents the reflection of a face, so a man's heart is reflected in the man himself" (Proverbs 27:19). The problem with this one, though, is that it requires such penetrating honesty with one's own inner person. I look at my own heart from the inside out. And if I am willing to search deeply and earnestly––albeit with some degree of pain––I can know my heart.

And what is worth knowing about one's heart? What are the things that allow you to see the real *you?* Here are a few indicators. You'll think of more.

• What do you think about most?

• What do you want more than anything else?

• Beyond the necessities, what do you spend money for?

From the Bible

Every good tree produces good fruit, but a bad tree produces bad fruit.

A good tree can't produce bad fruit; neither can a bad tree produce good fruit.

Every tree that doesn't produce good fruit is cut down and thrown into the fire. So you'll recognize them by their fruit.

MATTHEW 7:17-20

• What sort or style of humor makes you laugh?

• Who are the people you admire most, or the people whose company you enjoy most?

The beauty of asking these questions is that, if you have to distinguish between your immediate, honest answer and the one you think most proper to give, you know you're playing games. You can fool others, but you know your own heart. And you are aware that God knows it as well.

Only the man or woman who knows the real person within can set that true self before God. Socrates' "Know thyself" is more Christian than Greek, more spiritual than merely philosophical. "Test yourselves to make sure you are solid in the faith. Don't drift along taking everything for granted. Give yourselves regular checkups. You need firsthand evidence, not mere hearsay, that Jesus Christ is in you. Test it out. If you fail the test, do something about it" (2 Corinthians 13:5, *The Message*).

If you want to get in touch with the real you, listen to your heart.

Starting Right Now:
Answer these penetrating questions today—right here, right now. Get up from this place a real believer.

_____

_____

_____

_____

_____

_____

_____

_____

_____

_____

_____

_____

_____

_____

_____

_____

_____

_____

_____

_____

_____

_____

DUMB AND DUMBER

Sin comes with too high a price tag. You wind up selling your soul for a handful of trinkets and a few thrills, only to pay for it at a premium.

SOMETHING TO START WITH

I was driving home from my office a while back, listening to the radio. The fellow reading the news chuckled as he read the story of a man who robbed a convenience store clerk.

The thief apparently had a neat plan worked out. He would buy a pack of gum, give the clerk a $10 bill, and wait for her to open the cash drawer to make change. He would then grab all the money and bolt for the door. It worked. He got everything in the drawer and made a clean getaway, but with a grand total of $4.34. Since he left the clerk holding his ten dollars, he went in the hole to the tune of $5.66 for all his trouble!

The truth is that sin never delivers what it promises. It always returns less than we invest in self-esteem, integrity, and spiritual security. Need proof?

• Adam and Eve were promised freedom, wisdom, and life by Satan, only to be led to commit spiritual suicide.

• Sensuous Samson fell in love with a woman who did not love God and paid with his eyesight, his freedom, and eventually his life.

• Ananias and Sapphira were convinced they would be applauded as generous church members but wound up being buried as liars.

From the Bible

Humble yourselves...under the mighty hand of God, so that He may exalt you in due time, casting all your care upon Him, because He cares for you. Be sober! Be on the alert! Your adversary the Devil is prowling around like a roaring lion, looking for anyone he can devour. Resist him, firm in the faith, knowing that the same sufferings are being experienced by your brothers in the world.

1 PETER 5:6-9

In each of these biblical cases, sin promised something it could not deliver. And the same thing happens today.

• A "little white lie" that wouldn't hurt anybody has grown to such proportions that she can't even count all the other falsehoods that have been necessary to cover it.

• An e-mail invitation to an Internet porn site has turned into an addiction that has cost him not only huge amounts of money but also his self-respect.

• A well-deserved drink or joint at the end of a stressful day "just to unwind a bit" has become an obsession that makes everything else unimportant.

The lure of evil is the promise of quick pleasure without regard to long-term consequences. Truth and holiness are different. They often require self-denial for the sake of character, honor, and reward down the line.

When you're tempted, remember that somebody has fallen for a version of this before and paid a terribly high price. Juicy worms often hide some very sharp hooks.

"I'M HAPPY FOR YOU!"

One of the truest insights you can possess in evaluating your own character revolves around the following, selfless declaration: "I'm happy for you!"

SOMETHING TO START WITH

Politeness and good social form periodically dictate the statement, "*I'm happy for you!*" A colleague at work gets a promotion and raise. A friend announces his engagement. An acquaintance graduates from college, shows you her new car, or moves into a new house. Or you watch a total stranger win the big prize on "Who Wants to Be a Millionaire?" What is the tactful response? "*I'm happy for you!*"

To be able to say it and mean it shows that you have a generous spirit.

From the Bible

"May they all be one, just as You, Father, are in Me and I am in You. May they also be one in Us, so that the world may believe You sent Me.

"I have given them the glory that You have given to Me. May they be one just as We are one....

"I made Your name known to them and will make it known, so that the love with which You have loved Me may be in them, and I may be in them."

JOHN 17:21-22,26

To have to say it and *not* mean it reveals that you are being squeezed in the vise of envy and jealousy.

In the community of God, this is to be the operative rule: "Rejoice with those who rejoice; weep with those who weep" (Romans 12:15). Compassion toward someone in trouble seems to be easier than authentic joy over another's good fortune. The former allows us to feel secure, if not superior.

If it ever feels good to you that someone else has crashed and burned, you have a covetous heart and a cruel spirit. Worry about yourself. And pray for God to give you the power to get outside your too-egocentric world of resentment.

A man was jealous of an associate at his firm who moved into a new house much larger than his own. So he called a real estate agent, had his house listed for sale, and began searching for a nicer place. The very next day his eye was drawn to a listing that seemed to be everything he could want. So he called his agent to schedule an appointment for him to see it. He got the shock of his life when the agent said, "Why, that's our ad for the house you're living in now!"

The task of keeping up, moving ahead, or achieving status creates envy. Envy creates the next round of cutthroat competition. And conflict destroys personal peace. No less than the Apostle Paul admitted having to struggle against the sin of covetousness. Most of us are infected with the same spirit and have to struggle against the competitive spirit it generates.

Don't fall into the trap of comparing your situation with someone else's. Above all, when you learn of another's good fortune, tell him you're happy for him—and mean it.

Starting Right Now:
God has given us all more than we deserve. Think about what you do have instead of what you don't.

_____
_____
_____
_____
_____
_____
_____
_____
_____
_____
_____
_____
_____
_____
_____
_____
_____
_____
_____
_____
_____
_____
_____

WHEN CHARACTER TALKS

Some leaders are known for their persuasive words and inspiring eloquence.
Others are known for their integrity alone, which often sounds best unspoken.

SOMETHING TO START WITH

From 1949 to 1958, Pee Wee Reese was captain of baseball's Dodgers. Named not for his size but for playing marbles as a kid with a pee-wee shooter, he was a great shortstop, a daring baserunner, and a superb clutch hitter. He was an eight-time All-Star and sparked the Dodgers to seven National League pennants.

Throughout his playing days, Reese was respected as a person as well as a ballplayer. His fellow Dodgers called him simply "The Captain" and deferred to his judgment on many matters. He wasn't good at speeches. His leadership came from inner confidence, integrity, and consistency. His manner had the unpretentious effect of causing people to trust and follow him.

Just back from a three-year stint in the Navy during World War II, in which he had helped win a war against racial intolerance in Europe, Reese was soon to be caught up in fighting the same evil in his own country. His team owner had decided to break the barrier against black players by putting Jackie Robinson on the big-league roster.

Some of the Dodger players began circulating a petition in the clubhouse to protest the plan. It said in effect that the players signing it wouldn't play on a team with a black man. Confident that Reese would sign it because he was a Southerner, it was shoved under his nose. "I'm not signing!" he said, and the petition died.

From the Bible

When he arrived in Jerusalem, [Saul] tried to associate with the disciples, but they were all afraid of him….Barnabas, however, took him and brought him to the apostles and explained how, on the road, Saul had seen the Lord.

ACTS 9:26-27

Robinson was with the team for spring training in 1947. Before a game in Cincinnati, just across the river from Reese's native Kentucky, the ugliness was intense. Fans in the stands joined players in the opposing dugout to shout racial slurs at the solitary black man taking infield practice at second base.

Pee Wee raised his arm to halt the team's warmup. He walked from his shortstop position to second base and put his arm around Robinson's shoulders. That event is viewed as a turning point in the history of baseball--and by extension, a major blow against racism in America.

"Pee Wee kind of sensed the sort of hopeless, dead feeling in me and came over and stood beside me for a while," Robinson recalled. "He didn't say a word, but he looked over at the chaps who were yelling at me…and just stared. He was standing by me. I could tell you that."

Sometimes you don't need to say anything to lead. Just be there. Stand for what you know is right. There is an eloquence in actions that words can't equal.

Starting Right Now:
Where have you noticed injustice and unfairness in your world? Will you stand for it, or stand against it?

_____
_____
_____
_____
_____
_____
_____
_____
_____
_____
_____
_____
_____
_____
_____
_____
_____
_____
_____
_____
_____
_____
_____
_____

LITTLE HELP?

What a costly pride we harbor when we think the whole burden of the day rests on our shoulders. To share the load is not weakness, but wisdom.

SOMETHING TO START WITH

My calendar for this week looks pretty intimidating. Appointments, projects, presentations, and deadlines are scattered across it. And experience says that some of the most challenging things I'll face aren't even on my appointment book at all! They will come in the form of unexpected crises. Your expectations are probably similar.

Since neither of us has the option of erasing our calendars or swapping the week's plan for a mountain retreat, what's our best coping strategy? My plan is to approach it positively. I have no desire to run from responsibility or to trade serious effort for procrastination and idleness. Here's a thought that helps me, and perhaps it will have some meaning for you, as well:

From the Bible

So, what is Apollos? And what is Paul? They are servants through whom you believed, and each has the role the Lord has given. I planted, Apollos watered, but God gave the growth....

Now the one who plants and the one who waters are equal, and each will receive his own reward according to his own labor.

1 CORINTHIANS 3:5-6,8

A boy and his father were hiking a familiar path and enjoying their time together. As they negotiated a sharp turn in one of the narrower sections of their route, they came across a big rock that had turned loose, tumbled down the hillside, and come to rest dead center of their trail. Either it would have to be moved or they were blocked and would have to turn around and go home.

"Do you think I can move it?" asked the child.

"If you use all the strength you have," replied the father, "I'm sure you can."

So the young boy looked at the big stone, chose an angle of attack, and began pushing with all his might. He strained and grunted, summoning all the strength he had. He pushed and pushed. But the heavy rock refused to yield. With frustration obvious both on his face and in his voice, he turned to his dad and said, "You were wrong. I just can't do it."

Squatting beside him so he could look his son square in the face, the father smiled and said, "No, son. You just haven't used all your strength yet. I'm right here with you, and you haven't asked *me* to help!" Soon the path was clear. The two of them proceeded on what had appeared to the child to be a closed path.

Pride keeps some of us from asking another's aid. Then, when the barrier is still too great, we frequently forget that we haven't used all our strength until we have asked for the help of a loving Father who is standing nearby. "Give all your worries to him, because he cares for you" (1 Peter 5:7, *New Century Version*).

Suddenly my day doesn't look nearly so forbidding. How about yours?

Starting Right Now:
Scan the chicken-scratch of your daily planner. Which tasks could benefit from the help of others?

_____
_____
_____
_____
_____
_____
_____
_____
_____
_____
_____
_____
_____
_____
_____
_____
_____
_____
_____
_____
_____
_____

TAKE FIVE

You will never get around to all the things you want to do, could do, and should do until you learn the secret of making every minute count for good.

SOMETHING TO START WITH

"Take five!" someone says. And everybody in the room understands. The boss is stepping out to take a phone call. A technician has to change the lighting or rearrange the set. Everybody has been drinking coffee and needs a restroom break. So somebody gives permission to everyone present:

"Take five!"

Not a lot can be done in five minutes––even if we understand that the five-minute break may actually extend to ten, twenty, or more minutes. We're all still "standing by" to resume the project or meeting on short notice. We're not in control of the situation; we have a very limited time to grab another cup of coffee or make a phone call back to the office. You have to be deliberate with that time.

Come to think of it, though, a lot *can* be done with five minutes in a person's life. Consider these examples of what you could do in that brief time:

• Take five minutes to write a thank-you note to someone who did something thoughtful or helpful to you recently.

• Take five minutes to introduce yourself to someone you don't know.

• Take five minutes to listen to someone who has just had some positive thing happen in her life.

From the Bible

Jesus said, "I praise You, Father, Lord of heaven and earth, because You have hidden these things from the wise and the learned and revealed them to infants....

"Come to Me, all you who are weary and burdened, and I will give you rest. Take My yoke upon you and learn from Me, because I am gentle and humble in heart, and you will find rest for your souls."

MATTHEW 11:25,28-29

• Take five minutes to offer an ear to someone who seems discouraged and may need to talk about something that's troubling him.

• Take five minutes to watch a bird, study a leaf, or enjoy a sunset.

• Take five minutes to read a few lines from the Psalms and pray.

• Take five minutes to plan how you will affirm someone in your family when you get home from work tonight.

• Take five minutes to look deeply into your soul and forgive a real or imagined grievance or release an old grudge.

Time is the very essence of life. So using each day wisely and for some positive outcome is important. But we typically spend our days like our money--wastefully, in small increments here and there until it is all gone.

So is a five-minute increment out of this day too much to ask--more time than you will have to give? Probably not.

If you hear "Take five!" today, try one of these exercises. You might be amazed at the things you can accomplish in five minutes.

Starting Right Now:
Add to the list I've started with a personalized list of your own—and become a five-minute wonder.

_____
_____
_____
_____
_____
_____
_____
_____
_____
_____
_____
_____
_____
_____
_____
_____
_____
_____
_____
_____
_____
_____

A BIG HIT IN HEAVEN

A proper relationship with God requires two perspectives: 1) You don't deserve one ounce of God's grace; 2) He loves you too much to hold it back.

SOMETHING TO START WITH

Irving Berlin (1888-1989) had a unique career in American music. He wrote for both Broadway musicals and Hollywood films, and it was not unusual for his songs to be remembered and performed long after a show or movie had flopped. Although he typically wrote both the words and the music, he did not read music and could play the piano in only one key—F-sharp.

Here are just a few of Berlin's songs: "God Bless America," "Easter Parade," "Blue Skies," "A Pretty Girl Is Like a Melody," and "White Christmas." He wrote the musicals *Annie Get Your Gun* and *There's No Business Like Show Business.* Recognize him now?

In an interview for *The San Diego Union,* a creative reporter asked him this unconventional question: "Mr. Berlin, is there any question you've never been asked that you would like someone to ask you?"

"Well, yes, there is one," came the response. " 'What do you think of the many songs you've written that didn't become hits?' And my reply would be that I still think they are wonderful."

From the Bible

"Just as the Father has loved Me, I also have loved You. Remain in My love. If you keep My commandments you will remain in My love, just as I have kept My Father's commandments and remain in His love.

"I have spoken these things to you so that My joy may be in you and your joy may be complete....

"No one has greater love than this, that someone would lay down his life for his friends. You are My friends if you do what I command you."

JOHN 15:9-11,13-14

Some people need to be told that God takes great pleasure in them just because He made them in His own image. He thinks every single one of us is wonderful. It doesn't matter what anyone else thinks-- whether they see you as a "hit" or not, whether you've been acclaimed as a great success or written off by someone as a flop. God thinks you are awesome.

How can I be so sure of that, especially if I don't know your darkest secrets? King David said that human beings are only slightly lower in status than the angels that surround God's throne, and have been crowned with glory and honor by the Lord Himself (Psalm 8:5). If that isn't enough, "God proves His own love for us in that while we were still sinners Christ died for us!" (Romans 5:8). Case closed!

If you've been down on yourself lately, just remember the pleasure God takes in you—and bask in His affection. Why, if heaven had a refrigerator, your picture would be on its door. That's how wonderful He still thinks you are.

Starting Right Now:
Today's Christians talk freely about their sins, but not so often about the good things God is growing in them:

_____
_____
_____
_____
_____
_____
_____
_____
_____
_____
_____
_____
_____
_____
_____
_____
_____
_____
_____
_____
_____
_____

THAT'S "MISTER" TO YOU

He may be a bum on the street, an ingrate in the next cubicle, or a grump posing as a neighbor. Say hello to someone created in the image of God.

When Charles was still a boy, he worked in his father's warehouse. There were grown men working all around him. But his father wanted him to learn responsible work habits. And the adults kept a protective eye on him.

One of the men in the warehouse was (in the language of that time) an "old reprobate." He was known to cheat on his wife. He was anything but a virtuous fellow who deserved the respect--much less the imitation--of a teenaged boy. Even Charles sensed the man's wickedness and picked up on the lack of respect for the man among his own peers. So while everyone else in the boy's world was "Mr. Smith" or "Mr. Brown," the old scoundrel was simply "Joe."

Charles' dad heard his son speak to "Joe" one day and called the boy into his office. "Son," he began, "you know I've told you to address grown-ups respectfully. I heard you call out to 'Joe' a while ago, and I didn't like the sound of it."

So the son began explaining to his father why he made a deliberate distinction between "Joe" and "Mr. Brown." He ended by telling his father that the title "Mr." implied a degree of respect for someone that this man didn't deserve.

From the Bible

"You have heard that it was said, 'You shall love your neighbor and hate your enemy.' But I tell you, love your enemies, and pray for those who persecute you, so that you may be sons of your Father in heaven. For He causes His sun to rise on the evil and the good, and sends rain on the righteous and the unrighteous. For if you love those who love you, what reward will you have? Don't even the tax collectors do the same?"

MATTHEW 5:43-46

"You are going to treat that man properly, not because of who *he* is," said the father, "but because of who *you* are!" What a profound lesson for a parent to teach a child.

Did anyone teach you that certain behaviors are civil and polite? That being disrespectful reveals more about you than the object of your enmity? That you lower yourself in the eyes of virtuous people by being mean or hateful––even to someone who has done you wrong or merited your scorn?

Jesus taught His disciples to turn their cheeks to insults. He even warned about being persecuted for righteousness. But He never called His people to be unkind, rude, or disrespectful. *Take it from others, if you must, with courage and poise,* Jesus taught, *but never, ever be the one dishing it out!*

When you face provocation this week or feel the impulse to chide someone with rudeness or impudence, remember who you are and act accordingly.

Starting Right Now:
Radical obedience, radical measures. Try giving your best respect to the one who gets your goat the most.

_____
_____
_____
_____
_____
_____
_____
_____
_____
_____
_____
_____
_____
_____
_____
_____
_____
_____
_____
_____
_____
_____
_____

DUE DILIGENCE

How bold of an omnipotent God to entrust His creation into the care of mere mortals. How wasteful of us creatures to lazily forfeit the privilege.

SOMETHING TO START WITH

A country parson nearing the farm of one of his newest members could not help noticing the improvements the hardworking man had made in what had once been a poor piece of farm acreage.

Where there had once been dilapidated outbuildings, now he saw a new shed and a freshly painted barn. All the equipment was obviously being maintained well. The animals were healthy, and the fields were under cultivation. The place could hardly have looked better. So the preacher was determined to praise the farmer's hard work—being careful, of course, to acknowledge the hand of the Lord in it all.

"Russell, you and the Good Lord have worked wonders with this place!" he allowed. "I've not seen a better looking farm anywhere in the county this spring."

"Thank you, parson," said Russell, "but you should have seen what a disaster this place was when the Lord had the whole thing to Himself!"

By His precious grace, God gives human beings the power to identify with Him in exercising sovereignty over Planet Earth. And He wants us to be as earnest in our part of the task as He has been in His. Thus the book of Proverbs is filled

From the Bible

Remind them to be submissive to rulers and authorities, to obey, to be ready for every good work. . . . This saying is trustworthy. I want you to insist on these things, so that those who have believed God might be careful to devote themselves to good works. These are good and profitable for everyone. But avoid foolish debates, genealogies, quarrels, and disputes about the law, for they are unprofitable and worthless.

TITUS 3:1,8-9

with counsel about diligence. "Whoever works with a lazy hand becomes poor, but hard-working hands create wealth" (10:4). "Craving and having nothing—that is the appetite of lazy, while the appetite of the diligent is hale and hearty" (13:4). "The loafer does not plow in autumn; he looks at harvest time, and there is nothing" (20:4).

Work is not a curse, but unemployment or idleness is. Adam was to tend, subdue, and master the Garden of Eden. Yes, sin made Adam's task harder by virtue of the thorns and thistles it introduced into his environment. But work was part of the original and ideal arrangement of paradise.

Cervantes said, "Diligence is the mother of good fortune." Rather than envy the person who somehow manages to get by without hard work, pity him instead for having failed to develop a primary habit that is necessary to virtue.

God saves us by His lavish grace; that affirmation is good theology. People saved by grace partner with God in productive work; that behavior is noble character.

Starting Right Now:
Make sure you're busying yourself with the right things—long-lasting investments like these:

_____
_____
_____
_____
_____
_____
_____
_____
_____
_____
_____
_____
_____
_____
_____
_____
_____
_____
_____
_____

I BRAKE FOR RESPONSIBILITY

The next time you think you've outgrown your need to play by the rules, you'd better watch out! Life has a painful way of helping you remember.

Some people have a hard time with accountability and responsibility. They prefer to jump gates, break lines, and drive too fast. They think that they are exceptions to the rules and can get away with defying them. Then comes the moment of rude awakening. Reality breaks in. The piper has to be paid.

Take the strange anecdote of the Florida toll booth cheat as a costly case in point. Wesley Ridgwell saw no need to pay the paltry tolls along the Florida highways, so for ten months between August 1999 and June 2000, he zipped through 705 toll booths without paying.

From the Bible

Don't be deceived: God is not mocked. For whatever a man sows he will also reap, because the one who sows to his flesh will reap corruption from the flesh, but the one who sows to the Spirit will reap eternal life from the Spirit.

So we must not get tired of doing good, for we will reap at the proper time if we don't give up.

GALATIANS 6:7-9

When the 23-year-old man was first tracked down, he denied everything. "I'm such a good person," he protested. "People who know me just can't believe this is happening." He claimed that someone had stolen one of his two "JST CRZY" vanity license plates and put it on a car that looked like his. But his story fell apart when a police officer pulled over a car for not paying a toll. It bore the license plate "JST CRZY." And guess who was behind the wheel? You're ahead of me.

Ridgwell has a long history of traffic problems. A dozen convictions ranging from speeding to drunken driving are on his record. So this time, the court suspended his license for three months and fined him $15,000. Ouch! A couple of quarters here and there would have been far more bearable. "I apologize," he said. "I understand now that everyone should have to pay the tolls."

What taught *you* that lesson? Did you fudge your credentials and get into a job beyond your training and skills? Have you tried to make relationships work by taking without giving? What about professions of faith without a changed life?

Adam and Eve thought they could eat the forbidden fruit without paying the toll. David deemed himself a powerful enough man to take another man's wife and avoid the toll usually paid. Judas turned his back on Jesus and gave no thought to the toll he would have to pay for his choice.

Life makes its demands, from the dues we are expected to pay at toll booths to the moral consequences of our adult actions. Anyone who thinks he can escape life's toll booths is— "JST CRZY."

DON'T TRY THIS AT HOME

Do your family conversations usually center around chores to perform and expectations to meet? Bring your love home, not your laundry list.

SOMETHING TO START WITH

Most businesses are forced to think about efficiency. The elimination of waste not only improves the bottom line but typically makes the general work atmosphere better for everyone. Better organized tasks yield better results. But there are limits to this penchant for tighter organization that need to be respected.

The story goes that a particular efficiency expert closed his lecture to a group of employees with a warning. "Don't attempt these task-organizing tips at home," he said. "They only apply to the workplace."

One worker was intrigued. During the question-and-answer time, he raised his hand. "Why shouldn't we apply these things at home?" he asked.

With a bit of a blush on his face and some obvious discomfort with the question, the speaker shuffled his feet and cleared his throat. "My warning is rooted in my personal experience," he began. "I did a study of my wife's routine for fixing breakfast. I noticed that she made a lot of trips between the refrigerator and the stove, the table and the cabinets. And often she was carrying only one item. Finally, I told her what I had discovered

From the Bible

Do not owe anyone anything, except to love one another, for the one who loves another has fulfilled the law.

The commandments: "You shall not commit adultery, you shall not commit murder, you shall not steal, you shall not covet," and if there is any other commandment— all are summed up by this: "You shall love your neighbor as yourself."…Love, therefore, is the fulfillment of the law.

ROMANS 13:8-10

by applying my workplace skills to her methods. 'Honey, why don't you try carrying several things at once?' was the only suggestion I gave her. It seemed to make a lot of sense to me."

"Well," the questioner asked, "did it work? Did it save time?"

"Yes," the expert said. "It used to take her twenty minutes to get my breakfast. Now I can get my own in seven."

Did you ever discover that some tried-and-true methods of the office, factory, or store don't quite cut it at home? Families are built on relationships, not efficiency. Love and trust, not management techniques, are the cement of those connections. The same is true of healthy churches, for the role of their leaders is not to make them look more business-like but more Christ-like.

Your workplace may require you to schedule, regiment, and monitor others. But the people you love the most just need to know how precious they are to you.

God has accepted you with all your foibles and flaws; imitate Him by granting that grace to others.

THE MEASURE OF SUCCESS

It is so easy to forget what really matters in life. We tend to think that titles, power, and money make all the difference. But we tend to be mistaken.

SOMETHING TO START WITH

Many of us would like to have the position in the company, the athletic prowess, or the beauty that another has. So we set our life courses accordingly. We accumulate degrees and plaques. We focus on making more money. We starve and sweat to have a trim body.

Don't get me wrong! There's nothing intrinsically evil about any of these things. But are they the main ingredients to a life well-lived? Do they make a lasting difference? Will they have any value for eternity?

From the Bible

To those who are perishing the message of the cross is foolishness, but to us who are being saved it is God's power. For it is written: "I will destroy the wisdom of the wise, and I will set aside the understanding of the experts."…

Christ is God's power and God's wisdom, because God's foolishness is wiser than human wisdom, and God's weakness is stronger than human strength.

1 CORINTHIANS 1:18-19,24-25

Here's a little quiz that might help make the point I have in mind:

• Name the six wealthiest people in the world.

• Name the last five Academy Award winners for best actor and actress.

• Name the four most recent Heisman Trophy winners.

• Name the last three winners of the Miss America pageant.

• Name two people who won the top prize on "Who Wants to Be a Millionaire?"

My guess is that you weren't able to answer all five questions. Maybe even one! But these people are the best of the best in their fields. How quickly we forget things that seem so important at the time.

Now here's another quiz for you. See if you do any better on it:

• Name six teachers who helped you during your educational career.

• Name five people with whom you enjoy spending some of your free time.

• Name four personal heroes whose life stories have inspired you.

• Name three people who have helped you through a difficult time.

• Name two people you can always trust to honor a confidence.

I'll bet you did better generating answers to this set of questions than the first one. Why? The people who really matter in our lives aren't the ones with awards and money but the ones with character and compassion. Shouldn't this insight be instructive to all of us about what to pursue with our lives?

Don't climb the ladder of success only to find you've leaned it against the wrong wall. I think it was the late Erma Bombeck who once wrote: "Don't confuse fame with success. Madonna is one, and Helen Keller is the other."

Starting Right Now:
Do your thought patterns reveal that your life's goals are all about recognition, or about serving others?

_____
_____
_____
_____
_____
_____
_____
_____
_____
_____
_____
_____
_____
_____
_____
_____
_____
_____
_____
_____
_____
_____
_____

MAKING A LIST

There's more than one way to chart your daily course. Some will make you able to move mountains; others will make mountains out of mole hills.

I operate from daily to-do lists. Do you? Making out my list in a spiral-bound notebook not only helps me remember things that are ahead but also to prioritize them. Deadlines become their most menacing when you've let them get so close that they smother you into inactivity.

From the Bible

Don't worry about anything, but in everything, through prayer and petition with thanksgiving, let your requests be made known to God. And the peace of God, which surpasses every thought, will guard your hearts and your minds in Christ Jesus.

Finally, brothers, whatever is true, whatever is honorable, whatever is just, whatever is pure, whatever is lovely, whatever is commendable— if there is any moral excellence and if there is any praise— dwell on these things.

PHILIPPIANS 4:6-8

I try to keep my lists reasonably short, for as the number of items on my to-do list grows, the ability to manage my time effectively diminishes. The luxury of referring back to a list imposes discipline on my day and holds me to my tasks. "Planning is of no use at all," says Peter Drucker, "unless it eventually degenerates into work."

There are two other lists I keep as well. These aren't always written down in a notebook. Yet I carry them with me everywhere I go. And the strange thing is that each has the power to cancel out the other. One shrinks as the other grows.

• *My worry list* tends to be composed of things that are beyond my power to manage—crisis events, others' demands on me, and various things I'd like to bring under my control. These are the things that distract me during the day and keep me awake at night. They seldom generate productive activity of any sort, for the very idea that I can bring life under my personal control is only a delusion.

• *My prayer list* is made up of the people, situations, and events I choose to surrender to God. These are the things I *know* I can't handle. They are too big and too important for me to try to force them into an outcome I've settled in my mind.

See why these lists cancel out one another? Anything I've given over to God doesn't have to be fretted and sweated. He's competent enough to handle it. So long as I am trying to bring things under my personal control, though, I run the risk of fighting not only the defiant realities around me but God's will for my life. The more praying I do, the less power worry has to sap either my strength or my sleep.

The more items that get moved off your worry list and onto your prayer list, the better off you'll be. God will graciously replace your anxiety with His peace.

Starting Right Now:
Don't bother to add to your worry list today. Instead, use this space to craft today's prayer list.

_____
_____
_____
_____
_____
_____
_____
_____
_____
_____
_____
_____
_____
_____
_____
_____
_____
_____
_____
_____
_____
_____
_____

I BELIEVE I CAN FLY

Do you sometimes feel at the mercy of habits and patterns that fight with your faith and spoil your freedom? Christ is your ticket out of the torment.

SOMETHING TO START WITH

Merle Jordan writes about standing on the edge of the ocean, watching a young man and an older man row a small boat out to a larger one that was anchored at some distance from the shore. The older man climbed aboard, went to the wheel of the large boat, and brought its engine to life.

The young sailor's job was to hoist the anchor. Struggling with the heavy weight was no easy thing for him. But it was clear the boat was not about to move forward on its charted course until the anchor had been hauled aboard.

Jordan uses that episode as a metaphor for his book *Reclaiming Your Story*. He writes: "We are all anchored in the personal histories we inherit from a family of origin....Our maps of reality; images of God; values, beliefs, and meaning systems; patterns of relating, communicating, and interacting; sense of identity and self-worth; and emotional awareness and means of expression are largely determined by our relationships and experiences in our families of origin."

How on-target! Haven't you seen it play out in the life of someone you know? An abused child never learns to trust as an adult. Boys molested by men become aggressive to avoid feeling weak or afraid. Traumatized kids overreact to upsetting things with rage and horror. People who grew up with alcohol, violence, or aban-

From the Bible

From now on, then, we do not know anyone in a purely human way. Even if we have known Christ in a purely human way, yet now we no longer know Him like that.

Therefore if anyone is in Christ, there is a new creation; old things have passed away, and look, new things have come.

2 CORINTHIANS 5:16-17

donment issues tend to choose mates and business partners who have the same traits. After all, they can relate to them.

The Christian faith is about transformation. But some people never experience the new life Christ has made possible for them. And often it isn't their fault. They don't realize they are repeating history from their families of origin or from early life experiences. No one has helped them fathom that those lifelong patterns have them stuck in emotional cement.

If you have children, it is important that you look for and interrupt any unhealthy patterns in your family history. You don't want to pass them on to future generations. Your leadership in business, community, or church will also be enhanced through an awareness of how these dynamics work. You can become the catalyst for helping others find emotional and spiritual health.

We sometimes need others' help to pull up our anchors to the past in order to move forward on the journey God has in mind for us. Be brave. Hoist anchor!

Starting Right Now:
What holdovers from your past keep doing a number on your present? Identify them, then crucify them.

_____
_____
_____
_____
_____
_____
_____
_____
_____
_____
_____
_____
_____
_____
_____
_____
_____
_____
_____
_____
_____
_____

BURIED TREASURE

You'd think we'd learn. How many times have we been duped into believing that the gifts of God can be lightly sold and somehow yield a better return?

SOMETHING TO START WITH

According to a Court of Appeals panel, Martha Nelson's estate was a "victim of its own folly." The result of the ruling is that her heirs are not entitled to reclaim two paintings that were sold at auction to a couple in Tucson, Arizona, back in 1996. The couple paid $60 for the pieces and later sold them through Christie's auction house in New York for $1,072,000!

When Ms. Nelson died, her family put the two paintings on sale for a tiny fraction of their worth, unaware that *Magnolia Blossoms* and *Cherokee Roses* were valuable 19th-century works from noted artist Martin Johnson Heade. When the boondoggle was discovered, they brought suit to overturn the sale by arguing it was based on a mistake about the paintings' value.

A judicial panel ruled the estate representatives "had ample opportunity to discover what it was selling and failed to do so," acting to reclaim the paintings only after learning their true worth later. In effect the court said: *Sorry! You could have known; you should have known. It's too late now to recoup your gaffe.*

Esau did not trust God to honor the covenant promises he was due to inherit

From the Bible

See to it that no one falls short of the grace of God and that no root of bitterness springs up, causing trouble and by it, defiling many.

And see that there isn't any immoral or irreverent person like Esau, who sold his birthright in exchange for one meal. For you know that later, when he wanted to inherit the blessing, he was rejected because he didn't find any opportunity for repentance, though he sought it with tears.

HEBREWS 12:15-17

from Abraham and Isaac, so he sold his birthright to Jacob for a single meal. He wasn't the last to be so foolish:

• A teenager forfeits his or her chastity in the context of an immature relationship driven by lust; only later does that person realize how valuable an element of innocence and self-respect has been thrown away.

• A young couple just starting out chooses to strap themselves with impulsive and unwise debt; then come the bills in terms of both dollars and stress.

• A lie, an affair, abuse of one's body—we often don't see what valuable things we are trading for trifles.

As the court told Ms. Nelson's heirs, it is the possessors' duty to discern the value of things that are in their control. It is too late to call off a bad transaction after the fact.

Be very wise and discerning about the valuable things God has entrusted to you. There is little hope of reclaiming life's most valuable things after they have been traded for scraps.

Treating treasures like trash will come back to haunt you.

Starting Right Now:
Count your many blessings today. And tally up the cost of neglecting to keep them in good condition.

DARE TO BE STUPID

The first time anything new and creative is proposed, it gets labeled. And the tag that's usually placed on these novel ideas gives it little chance of flying.

SOMETHING TO START WITH

Can't you just hear it? *Let me get this straight, Orville. You and Wilbur are building a machine that will do what? Heavier-than-air flying machines are the stupidest hoax anybody ever palmed off on gullible boys like you Wrights. Get a real job!*

Or maybe it was somebody's harebrained idea of talking pictures, or black and white children attending the same school, or men walking on the moon. More than one person was berated for giving voice to such "silly" ideas.

It turns out that some of the people who dared to propose such outlandish possibilities are now regarded as geniuses. Revolutionaries. Heroes. And it was only because they dared to question others and to question themselves. They challenged the limitations others were willing to take for granted.

From the Bible

[Jesus] went into a house, and the crowd gathered again so that they were not even able to eat. When His family heard this, they set out to restrain Him, because they said, "He's out of His mind."

And the scribes who had come down from Jerusalem said, "He has Beelzebul in Him!" and "He drives out demons by the ruler of the demons!"

MARK 3:20-22

There is something in your profession or business, your family or church that could be done better. A situation could be more productive. A relationship could be healthier. An objective could be clarified. Some lofty ideal to which all in the group give lip service could actually be implemented. But I will warn you up front: Like restoring an old house, it will take twice as long as you thought, cost far more than you anticipated, and strain every important relationship in your life.

So you will have to be the one to decide if it is worth it to undertake something so ambitious and costly. There will be false starts. There will be embarrassing mistakes along the way. But the potential outcome could be as important to your personal situation as the achievements of the Wright brothers, Rosa Parks, and Neil Armstrong were to their time and place.

The problem with our world is not that there are no more frontiers to challenge and conquer. There are too few explorers--too few people willing to ask obvious questions and challenge traditional wisdom, too few of us wanting to take risks that could make us look…stupid.

With no irreverence intended, I'm certain people used the term of Jesus. They called him demon-possessed and crazy, a blasphemer and insurrectionist. And all because he dared to question conventional wisdom and practices.

If you are fortunate enough to have a dream in your heart, be willing to make mistakes in pursuit of it. Dare to be stupid. You just might change your world.

Starting Right Now:
You're waiting for…what? You know what God is telling you to do. What are you going to do about it?

_____
_____
_____
_____
_____
_____
_____
_____
_____
_____
_____
_____
_____
_____
_____
_____
_____
_____
_____
_____
_____
_____
_____
_____

HUNGER PAINS

Line your personal birdcage as extravagantly as you want. But life can make a mess of the Sunday comics just as fast as the Tuesday classifieds.

A fellow who had grown tired of living alone went to a pet store to buy a parrot. He thought the bird might fill some of his lonely hours. The very next day, however, he came back to complain, "My new bird doesn't talk."

The store owner asked if he had a mirror in the bird's cage, and the man said he didn't. "Oh, parrots love mirrors," he explained. "When he sees his reflection in the mirror, he'll just start talking away." So he sold him a birdcage mirror.

But the bird owner was back the next day, griping that his parrot still hadn't said a word. "That's very peculiar," allowed the pet expert. "How about a swing? Birds really love these little swings, and a happy parrot is a talkative parrot." So the man bought a swing, took it home, and installed it in the cage.

He was back the next day with the same story. "Does he have a ladder to climb?" the salesman asked. "That just has to be the problem. Once he has a ladder, he'll probably talk your ear off!" So the fellow bought a ladder.

But again, the man was back at the pet store when it opened the next day. From the look on his face, the owner knew something was wrong. "Didn't your parrot like the ladder?" he asked. His

From the Bible

"Blessed are the poor in spirit, because the kingdom of heaven is theirs.

"Blessed are those who mourn, because they will be comforted.

"Blessed are the gentle, because they will inherit the earth.

"Blessed are those who hunger and thirst for righteousness, because they will be filled."

MATTHEW 5:3-6

repeat customer looked up and said, "Well, the parrot died."

"I'm so sorry," the stunned business-man said. "Did he ever say anything?"

"Yes. He finally talked just before he died. In a weak little voice, he asked me, 'Don't they sell any bird seed at that pet store?'"

Some of us have mistakenly thought that happiness consists of lining our cages with toys, gadgets, and other stuff. Excessive consumption has become the hallmark of American life. But there is a spiritual hunger in the human heart that can't be satisfied by seeing one's own image reflected back in vanity mirrors, playing with our grown-up toys, or climbing the corporate ladder. Our hearts need real nourishment.

The love of family and friends, relationships over the pursuit of more things, personal integrity, a secure connection to God--these are the things that feed the soul.

Have you chosen a life course that leads to a destination that matters?

Starting Right Now:
What is your current ratio of permanent possessions to throwaway treasures? Try counting and see:

_____

_____

_____

_____

_____

_____

_____

_____

_____

_____

_____

_____

_____

_____

_____

_____

_____

_____

_____

_____

_____

_____

OLYMPIC GLORY

I don't know what your favorite story of athletic achievement is. But pretty soon, this one will be among your most memorable Olympic experiences.

SOMETHING TO START WITH

Kay Poe and Esther Kim have been best friends since they were seven years old. Among other things they have in common, the two young ladies from Houston both compete at the highest levels in taekwondo. In fact, they both advanced to the finals in the Women's Olympic Flyweight division at the 2000 U.S. Olympic Team Trials.

What a classic story was unfolding! Reporters and photographers were poised to record the outcome of so intense a competition between two girls who had been close for so long. But a sports story would soon be overshadowed by a far more important friendship story.

Kay had dislocated her left kneecap in her semi-final match of the round-robin tournament. Though ranked number one in the world at her sport, it was questionable that she could compete against her best friend. Being barely able to stand as the final match approached, it became a foregone conclusion that Esther would win, travel to the 2000 Olympic Games in Sydney, and represent the United States in the international competition these two had worked toward for so long.

From the Bible

My defense to those who examine me is this: Don't we have the right to eat and drink? Don't we have the right to be accompanied by a Christian wife, like the other apostles, the Lord's brothers, and Cephas? Or is it only Barnabas and I who have no right to refrain from working?…If others share this authority over you, don't we even more?

However, we have not used this authority; instead we endure everything so that we will not hinder the gospel of Christ.

1 CORINTHIANS 9:3-6,12

But on the day of the match, Esther Kim shocked the crowd by forfeiting the match to Kay rather than defeat her friend in an unfair competition. And in the process, she won a personal battle over ego and selfishness. Amidst frequent stories of cheating and taking unfair advantage in order to win at any price, Esther showed how to win by losing.

"Even though I didn't have the gold medal around me," said Esther, "for the first time in my life, I felt like a real champion." Her generosity of spirit was honored with the Citizenship Through Sports Award and with an all-expenses-paid trip to the 2000 Olympic Games from the International Olympic Committee.

Paul wrote about giving up certain "rights" for the sake of people he loved. Parents do it all the time for their children. And occasionally friends make magnanimous gestures like Esther's.

The next time you are inclined to bemoan the selfishness of the masses, recall this story of a young athlete's largess—and rise to the level of her example.

Starting Right Now:
Could you perform the equivalent of this young fighter's sacrifice for a friend you care about?

LIVING YOUR DASH

Between now and the day they etch a final date on your cemetery stone, you have daily opportunities to make sure your life speaks of eternity.

SOMETHING TO START WITH

A friend of mine shared a poem with me recently—not a piece of classic literature, mind you, but several thought-provoking lines about living one's "dash." You know what a person's dash is? It's that little fragment of a line between the years of someone's birth and death. Here's how it's written in text or on grave markers: "Shirley Jane Doe (1945–2000)."

From the Bible

I am already being poured out as a drink offering, and the time for my departure is close. I have fought the good fight, I have finished the race, I have kept the faith.

In the future, there is reserved for me the crown of righteousness, which the Lord, the righteous Judge, will give me on that day, and not only to me, but to all those who have loved His appearing.…

To Him be the glory forever and ever! Amen.

2 TIMOTHY 4:6-8,18

That tiny, nondescript dash stands for everything she ever was or did. It covers all her accomplishments and fears, all her accumulations and losses, everything that made anybody notice and care that she ever lived at all.

For it matters not how much we own:
The cars…the house…the cash,
What matters is how we live and love
And how we spend our dash.

This anonymous poem reminds me of a sermon by an African-American preacher I heard years ago. He read Mark 4:35-36 and told how Jesus and his disciples launched their boat on the Sea of Galilee. Then he read Mark 5:1 that tells how the little group went "to the other side of the sea." He titled his sermon "Between the Launch and the Landing."

The material he omitted tells of a "fierce windstorm" that nearly "swamped" their boat. It tells of the disciples' fear as Jesus slept in the stern and of the miracle that happened when Jesus rebuked the storm and said, "Peace! Be still!"

Between the launch and landing of every life, between the date of your birth and death, there will be storms, fears, and failures. But there will also be those occasional triumphs of faith. You will call out to the Lord, and He will be there!

If we treat each other with respect,
And more often wear a smile…
Remembering that this special dash
Might only last a little while…

The poem closes with a reminder that everyone is writing her or his own eulogy every day.

Would you be proud
Of the things they say
About how you spent your dash?

Life doesn't promise smooth sailing, but those who travel with Jesus on board are guaranteed a safe landing. So how are you living your dash?

Starting Right Now:
What do you promise to start doing today that others will remember about you tomorrow?

_____
_____
_____
_____
_____
_____
_____
_____
_____
_____
_____
_____
_____
_____
_____
_____
_____
_____
_____
_____
_____
_____
_____
_____

NOTES

More ONE MINUTE BIBLES

Men of Character
0-8054-9267-4

Women of Character
0-8054-9277-1

Men in Leadership
0-8054-9153-8

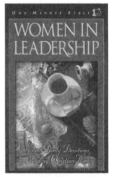

Women in Leadership
0-8054-9193-7

90 Days in the Word for Business Professionals
0-8054-9363-8

90 Days with the Christian Classics
0-8054-9278-X

One Minute Bible for Starters
0-8054-9386-7

One Minute Bible for Students
0-8054-9348-4

One Minute Bible Devotions for Kids
0-8054-9297-6

The Guy Who Lost His Beach House
0-8054-9398-0

The Kid Who Would Be King
0-8054-9399-9

If you would like to receive
The FAX of Life
by e-mail every Monday morning,
send a subscription request to
RShelly@woodmont.org
and type "Subscribe" in the message area.

This is a free service, and your e-mail address
will not be shared with any other originator
of electronic mail.